The Flesh of God

The Flesh of God

A Study
of the
Infancy Narratives

by

Steve Kellmeyer

Bridegroom Press
Peoria, IL

www.bridegroompress.com
info@bridegroompress.com

Nihil obstat: Msgr. Stephen P. Rohlfs, Censor Librorum.
Imprimatur: Most Reverend Daniel R. Jenky,
Catholic Diocese of Peoria.

The *nihil obstat* and *imprimatur* are official declarations that a book is free of doctrinal and moral error. No implication is contained herein that those who have granted the nihil obstat and imprimatur agree with the content, opinions, or statements expressed.

ISBN: 0-9718128-0-2

Printed in the United States of America

Contents

Introduction

Society does strange things with holy days, now called holidays. A century ago, Advent had a distinct place in the secular world. Christmas preparations did not begin until the first Sunday of Advent, Christmas trees and assorted Christmas items were not put up until Christmas season began, that is, on Christmas Eve. Christmas season proper, the twelve days between Christmas Day and the Feast of the Epiphany (the visit of the Magi), was the time for small gift giving and celebration, as one might guess from the song "The Twelve Days of Christmas."

This all changed sixty years ago, as the winds of World War II swept young men thousands of miles from home and into the battlefield. Anxious parents wanted their boys to have some reminders of Christmas at the front, and everyone knew it took at least six weeks to transit anything across the Atlantic via troop ship. As a result, the demand for Christmas items during the war years began to peak well before Advent had actually begun. The necessities of war have now become a necessity of the marketplace. What was once All Holy Eve is now Halloween and Halloween now marks the beginning of what passes for Advent. Advent is treated as Christmas season. Christmas season proper is gone entirely. When was the last time anyone had a school Christmas pageant or business Christmas party *after* Christmas Day? Everyone is too tired and overspent (in every sense of the word), to celebrate. Our future-oriented society celebrates the expectation, not the event or the joy that follows it.

The essence of Catholic life is, however, living in the reality and inviting others to live there as well. This means we have an obligation to change the culture. Unfortunately, we cannot reach our goal if we do not have a proper understanding of that goal.

This Scripture study is designed to place things back into their proper perspectives. It fills the Advent and Christmas seasons as nearly as possible with a steady contemplation of the story of the birth of Christ. The infancy narratives are a gold-mine of information about the life of Christ and the life of the Church. Because the Incarnation is the central event in human history, the events of the infancy narratives ripple throughout all of time. Like a stone thrown into a quiet pool, the impact of the Incarnation sends its ripples both backward, into the history preceding the event, and forward, right down into this day. When we read the

Scriptures with this understanding in mind, we can find the "ripples" which point to the Incarnation both in the Old Testament and in the New. In fact, every event and person of the Old Testament points to some kind of fulfillment in the New Testament, every event and person in the New Testament finds its meaning in the Gospels, the life of Jesus.

This is the guiding interpretive principle of Catholic Bible study. In this study, we will be looking for the New Testament hidden in the Old, and the Old Testament revealed in the New. We will expect every name, every event, to have not only a literally true meaning - each event actually occurred - but also a meaning which points beyond itself to the eternal divine. In this way, the Scripture study will mirror the purpose of the liturgical year it follows.

How to Use This Book

The first two chapters of Luke and the first two chapters of Mark contain the infancy narratives. Together, they form the basis for everything we know about the events surrounding the birth of Christ. Depending on how much time you have available, you can work through these four chapters in one of two ways.

If your schedule leaves you with something like an hour a week to undertake Scripture study, then use the first section of this book, "Weekly Scripture Study." It contains seven sessions, which will allow you to cover the four weeks of Advent and the twelve days of Christmas at the rate of roughly one session a week.

If, on the other hand, you believe you can devote roughly twenty to thirty minutes a day to Scripture study, use the second section of the book, "Daily Scripture Study." It contains thirty-two sessions, which will allow you to cover roughly six sessions a week over the same time period. This gives you at least one day a week to make up for the unscheduled emergencies that are so popular at this time of year. Both sections cover the same four chapters from Scripture and roughly the same topics, although the daily study obviously has room for more detail than the weekly study does. The description below addresses the daily sessions, but the weekly sessions follow essentially the same format.

In both the weekly and the daily study portions of the book, the work is divided into five major sections: the four weeks of Advent and the Christmas season, each with a different theme. For the "weekly study," not much more needs to be said about the divisions. In the "daily study" portion of the book, each of the themes is divided into several easily accomplished daily sessions. Whereas each of the seven weekly sessions covers roughly thirty verses at a time, each individual session in the daily study covers roughly five verses. The first three weeks of Advent each has six sessions, the fourth week of Advent has four sessions; Christmas season has ten sessions. The themes and sessions are divided as follows:

1st week of Advent:	John is Announced (6 days)
2nd week of Advent:	Angel Appears to Mary (6 days)
3rd week of Advent:	Angel Appears to Joseph (2 days)
	John is Born (4 days)
4th week of Advent:	Jesus is Born (4 days)
Christmas Season:	Visit of the Wise Men (2 days)
(12 days in length)	Innocents Slaughtered (2 days)
	Mary/Jesus Purified (4 days)
	Finding in the Temple (2 days)

For both weekly and daily sessions, every session header lists the theme title, the total verses covered under that theme, and the specific verses being studied for that day's session. As an added bonus for those who use the daily session, daily session headers also inform the reader of the feast days of the Church which are associated with that week's theme. In both the weekly and daily sessions, the header is followed by a list of paragraph numbers from the *Catechism of the Catholic Church* and Scripture references. That, in turn, is followed by a general commentary and a short question list.

Advent and Christmas seasons are busy seasons. Thus, each session can be completed in twenty to thirty minutes by simply reading the three or four verses under study, reading the general commentary and answering the questions. If you have time, studying the additional Scripture references and the *Catechism* references will very much enrich your understanding. The more thought and prayer you put into each week's session, the more treasures you will find buried in its field.

Except for the Bible itself, the *Catechism* is the most important book a Catholic can own. It, together with Scripture, contains everything Catholics believe. Nearly every paragraph in the *Catechism* contains some kind of Scripture reference. The *Catechism's* use of Scripture helps us understand what Scripture means. Thus, each Scripture session lists all the *Catechism* paragraphs that directly reference the verses under study. While each day's session subject may be discussed in other *Catechism* paragraphs as well, the only paragraphs listed are those which directly reference the Scripture verses under study for that session. This keeps each session to a manageable length.

This study is much more useful when the day's individual *Catechism* paragraph numbers are read. If you have more time, you are strongly urged to use the *Catechism's* table of contents, its index, and the paragraph number cross-references in the left and right margins of each *Catechism* page to research more deeply. On occasion, the verses under study won't have a corresponding *Catechism* reference – this is true of our first session, in fact. Keep in mind that the topic discussed is often still present in the *Catechism*.

Old and New Testament Scripture references are listed after *Catechism* references. Nearly every verse in the infancy narratives is meant to recall another verse somewhere in the Old or New Testament. So, each Scripture reference line in this study will begin with number of the infancy narrative verse we are studying. This is followed by a short description of the theme of the other Scripture verse(s) it is calling to mind, and a list of those verses. While a short explanation of these other verses is almost always included in the explanation for the day, it is certainly a good idea to look up some or all of them if time allows. When doing so, be sure to read the verses before and after it. This will give a better feel for the context of the words the Gospel writer or his eyewitnesses want to recall to the reader. Thus, if Luke 1:1-4 refers to 1 Cor 15:3, we should look up 1 Cor 15:3, but begin reading somewhere near the end of 1 Cor 14 and continue reading a few verses past 1 Cor 15:3, so as to get a better idea of what 1 Cor 15:3 means. This will help us understand how it relates to Luke 1:1-4.

The general commentary is kept to a minimum. In order to keep session time manageable, many ideas and general concepts are only briefly outlined, pointing out aspects which the casual reader might otherwise easily miss. The general commentary tends to rely heavily on a concept called "typology," a manner of reading Scripture common to all Christians until the Reformation in the 1500's. It is not necessarily an obvious way of reading Scripture, but it is quite useful.

Each session has between four and six questions. These questions are primarily meant to help you remember what you have just read, although some of the questions will ask you to think about concepts that are not covered in the explanation.

The last question often refers to the *Catechism* references at the beginning of the day' study. As with Scripture, it is useful to read the *Catechism* paragraphs that precede and follow any paragraph number listed in a particular session.

If, as a result of this study, you want to learn more about the "Liturgy of the Hours", contact a consecrated person in your local parish or look on the Web for more information. John Paul II recommends this prayer strongly to all Christians, as it is an easy way to learn the Scriptures quickly and a wonderful way to pray them.

Weekly
Scripture Study

John the Baptist Announced
1st Sunday of Advent
Luke 1:1-25

Catechism references to Luke 1:1-25
332: Angel in the divine plan
523: St. John the Baptist
696: Fire and the Spirit
716: The people of the poor
717: A man sent by God
718: The new Elijah
724: Mary and the Holy Spirit
1070: What is liturgy?
2684: The communion of saints

In Luke 1:1-4, we see Luke laying the foundation for his Gospel account, an account which actually has two parts. Luke wrote both the Gospel named for him and the Acts of the Apostles, intending the two to be read together as one story. Indeed, if you compare Luke 1:1-4 with Acts 1:1-5, Luke himself tells us this.

Luke's opening Gospel passage tells us several things. We discover that many people who were not eyewitnesses, including Luke, are compiling accounts of the life of Jesus based on the testimony of still-living eyewitnesses. Luke is writing "an orderly account" to Theophilus, whose Greek name literally means "One who loves God." So, what can we take away from the first four verses of the Gospel of Luke? We know that this Gospel is based on eyewitness accounts, we know that God intends this Gospel account to be orderly, so that we may better comprehend it, and we know that it is addressed to the one who loves God. In a very real sense, God is speaking to each one of us here, establishing his credentials with us, demonstrating his love and the care that He takes in order to make sure that we will have a very clear idea about Him and His relationship to us.

The first thing a careful reader will be struck by are the details Luke supplies. He tells us the words of the conversation between the angel and Zechariah while they were together in the temple as Zechariah burned incense. During this time, Zechariah was alone – he had been "chosen by lot." This means Luke had to have interviewed Zechariah to find out the particulars of the story. Likewise, the conversations he records between Mary and Gabriel were intimate conversations, known only to those two. Mary must have related these details to Luke, for no one else would know them. Indeed, many Scripture scholars have noted that the first two chapters of Luke are written in a Greek that is stylistically quite different from the rest of the Gospel. The first two chapters actually appear to be a translation of an account from another language into Greek. This is not surprising when we remember that Mary and Zechariah undoubtedly spoke Aramaic as their first language – Luke is giving us their accounts in their own words, translating their Aramaic directly into the Greek.

Notice also the importance of details in this historical account; for instance, consider the detail that Zechariah was chosen by lot. Being chosen by lot was not an unusual method of choosing successors or dividing up property (see Numbers 26:55 or Judges 20:9, for example). This method of choosing will be seen again in Acts 2:23-26 when Luke describes how Matthias was chosen over Barsabbas to become the apostle who replaces Judas. But if we read Numbers 26:55 or Numbers 33:54, we discover that the use of lot was the key to inheritance. When the Promised Land was divided up among the Twelve tribes, it was divided by lot. Thus, Zechariah's being chosen by lot for the Temple worship is a sign that a new inheritance is coming.

Zechariah was the priest chosen to burn incense in the Temple. The Jews burned incense for two reasons, one of which they realized, and a second which they did not. The Jews knew the smoke of incense represented the prayers of all the faithful, rising up to God as a pleasing aroma before Him. This is why the whole people prayed outside the temple at the hour of incense – the actions within were actively linked with the actions outside. What they did not realize was that the thurimer (or censor), in which the incense burned, was itself a symbol of the Incarnation God was about to accomplish. The censor in which the burning coal is contained represents Jesus' human nature, the burning coals inside it represent the divine nature of God, who is a consuming fire (Hebrews 12:29). Thus, when Christians use the censor we are reminded that all of our prayers rise to God only through Jesus Christ, the one mediator between God and man (1 Timothy 2:5). This is why it is most appropriate to use the censor during Mass and Eucharistic benediction. The incense and the thurimer are symbolic representations of Christ and His mediation, tied together as the prayers and the incense were at the Temple.

This Eucharistic connection is more firmly established in two different ways: first, Zechariah's family was the eighth of the 24 groups of Levitical priests (1 Chronicles 24:7-19). Jesus, the first Apostle and our High Priest (Hebrews 3:1), rose one day after the seventh (sabbath) day, that is, He rose on the eighth day (Sunday). His priesthood is thus symbolically linked to the Resurrection. Second, the angel appeared to Zechariah near the altar, the place of sacrifice. From that location, Gabriel announced the preparations for the coming of the True High Priest. He says God will bestow exceptional holiness on John, who will lead many to salvation, and whose whole life prepares the Messiah's way. "John" means "God is gracious." As Paul reminds us in 1 Cor 3:9, we are God's co-workers. Through the prophets of the Old Testament and through Zechariah and John the Baptist, God graciously allows men to prepare His way. Luke lays this groundwork here and he intends us to remember this, for in Luke 7:26-27, he will remind us that Jesus links the prophecy of Malachi 3:1 to John's coming.

Gabriel's own name is also important, for it means "might of God." Notice how differently the might of God will treat Zechariah as opposed to Mary (Luke 1:18-23, Luke 1:34-38). This difference is based on the different understandings they displayed: Zechariah *doesn't believe* God can give life through the marital act he performs with his wife. Mary doesn't disbelieve, she simply *doesn't understand* how she could become pregnant given that she has never undertaken the marital act (verse 34). Disbelievers are silenced, while those who are confused are enlightened.

Note finally that both Zechariah and Elizabeth hold privileged positions in the nation of Israel: Elizabeth descends from Aaron, Moses' brother (Exodus 4:27). Aaron performed all the miracles in front of Pharoah and was himself the first high priest, anointed by Moses himself. Zechariah is a Levitical priest. As Matthew 1:7 shows, Abijah, Zechariah's forefather, is the great-grandson of David and also a forefather of Jesus. Yet, though Luke tells us the lineages of both Zechariah and Elizabeth are noble, Luke follows this by telling us something even more important: both Elizabeth and Zechariah were righteous and blameless. What Luke says about them reminds us of what the apostle Paul will tell us about himself in 1 Corinthians 4:3-5 and Phillippians 3:4-6. Thus, there is some irony in the fact that Elizabeth sees her own pregnancy as the Lord's way of taking away her reproach among men (Luke 1:25). Zechariah cannot tell her, so she does not yet fully realize that her pregnancy has much more importance than simply stopping wagging tongues.

Jesus Announced to Mary & Joseph
2nd Sunday of Advent
Luke 1:26-56 and Matthew 1:1-25

Catechism references to Luke 1:26-56, Matthew 1:1-25

64: Work of the prophets	148: Mary, obedience, faith
269: The Holy Spirit	273: God's power
276: Scripture & God's power	332-333: Angelic work
422: God sent His Son	430: Jesus – "God saves"
437: The Shepherds	448: Lord Jesus
452: The name of Jesus	484: The Annunciation
486: The Christ	488: Mary's predestination
490-491: ImmaculateConception	494-495: Obedience of Faith
497: Jesus' virginal conception	505: Our birth as sons of God
510: Mary's perpetual virginity	523: St. John the Baptist
559: Jesus' Messianic entrance	697: Symbols of cloud/light
706: Spirit of promise	709: Kingdom and Exile
717: John, precursor	722-723: Mary, full of grace
744: Preparing God's coming	971: All call her blessed
1507: Heal the sick	1846: Mercy and Sin
2097: Adoration	2465: God, source of all truth.
2571: Abraham and faith	2599: Jesus prays
2617: The prayer of Mary	2619: The Magnificat
2675-2677: Mary's unique work	2807: Hallowed be thy name
2812: God revealed in Jesus	2827: Worshippers of God
2856: Amen	

Short commentary on Luke:

As we see in Luke 1:26, the angel appears to Mary while Elizabeth is in her sixth month. Through this notation, we begin to understand that Elizabeth and Mary are linked: what happens to one prefigures what will happen to the other. When we realize this, Luke 1:24 from the previous week suddenly stands out in bright contrast. Elizabeth shows her humility for the great miracle done within her by hiding herself, through this action, she prefigures the immense humility of Mary.

Likewise when we reach Luke 1:28, we begin to see an enormous contrast on a number of levels. First, while the angel who prophesied John's appearance comes to Zechariah, Elizabeth doesn't see an angel. Angels, however, will appear to both Joseph and Mary. Mary is thus marked off as a particularly special woman. This marking is further reinforced by the angel's greeting to Mary. Although Elizabeth and Zechariah are both descendants of noble lineage, Mary's lineage is not clearly given, yet despite this lack of evidence for noble lineage, Mary is greeted by the angel with the words: "Hail, full of grace!" The word used for "Hail!" – chairoo - is a royal greeting. This word is used only six times in Scripture: Matthew 26:48-49, where Judas betrays Jesus, Mark 15:18, John 19:3, and Matthew 27:29, where Roman soldiers mock Jesus' kingship, and Matthew 28:8-9, when the risen Jesus addresses the women outside the tomb. Judas uses the term in order to help convince the Roman soldiers that Jesus wants to be a temporal king, and the soldiers mock him with the term for the same reason. Jesus uses it to address the women after the Resurrection, because through His Resurrection they have become a royal priesthood, a holy nation, a people set apart (1 Peter 2:9). But the angel uses the word to address someone who we do not know is even of noble human lineage. The only king an angel recognizes is God. Why would he address a human person with a royal title? Because in Israel, it is not the wife of the king who is the queen, rather, it is the mother of the king. The angel addresses Mary as the Queen Mother of God, who will be her son.

The angel follows this word with the title "full of grace" – unique in Scripture. Through this acclamation, we are brought to realize that Mary has been immaculately conceived, conceived in the fullness of grace, without any of that lack of grace which we know as sin. She is the first normal human being brought into existence since Adam and Eve were formed by the hand of God, the first since them to have the full measure of grace which every human is supposed to have, but which none of us do, because of original sin. Mary, a daughter of Abraham and David, fulfills the prophecies made to both of them (Genesis 12:3 and 2 Samuel 7:12-16), while also, in her visit to Elizabeth, fulfilling the prophecy made by the angel to Zechariah in Luke 1:15.

Incidentally, two important prayers of the Church and part of a third are found in this section of Luke: the Magnificat, which every consecrated person must pray every day, is in Luke 1:46-55, the Angelus is based on Luke 1:26-39, while the first half of the Hail Mary is found in Luke 1:26-42.

Short commentary on Matthew:

In Jesus' geneology, Matthew reminds us that four of the women - Tamar, (Genesis 38, 1 Chronicles 2:4), Rahab (Joshua 2:6,17), Bathsheba (2 Samuel 11:12,24) and Ruth – were foreigners, some with rather disreputable characters. Through this geneology, Matthew reminds us that God intends to save all men. Further, if by referring to Isaiah 7:14 and remembering the prophecy of a painless birth made in Isaiah 66:6, we find a small part of the beginning of the doctrine of Mary's perpetual virginity: virgin before, during and after the birth of Jesus.

However, Matthew, through his reporting of the angel's words, reminds us that Joseph is of David's line (1:20). That is, Joseph will assist in the fulfillment of the promises God made to David. Note that man gives names in very few places in Scripture. He does so in Genesis, for the animals, and God directs the giving of a name in the New Testament only to Zechariah, Mary and Joseph. When Joseph "called his name Jesus" (Matthew 1:25), he was by that act declaring his true fatherhood of Jesus, not in the biological sense, but in the sense that Joseph will care for Jesus, helping his human nature be conformed to God. Pope John Paul II tells us that our biological parenthood is only the beginning of the work of parenting – it is perfected only in how we bring our children to full understanding of God. Though Jesus always knew He was God, still there was a way in which Joseph truly helped Him grow in His human knowledge so that it was capable of always fully understanding His own divinity.

Some mistakenly think the word "until" in Matthew 1:25 shows Joseph did have marital relations with Mary after Jesus' birth. For the Hebrews, however, no such meaning was intended. In Genesis 8:5, the waters receded "until the mountain tops were seen." and in 1 Corinthians 15:25 Jesus reigns "until all enemies are under his feet." In both of those passages, "until" simply describes an important event in an on-going process. What happens after the event is no different than what happened before. Similarly, the "until" here does not indicate that Joseph had relations with Mary after the birth of Jesus, nor does any other passage of Scripture lend credence to the idea. Even the phrase "brothers of Christ", common to the New Testament, is used to mean "cousins", not biological brothers. Hebrew, which is a tribal language, has no word for brother. Any two people descended from the same patriarch (e.g., Levi, Benhamin, Judah, etc.) were considered to be of the same family.

For Further Study:
Would you like to read more about Gabriel? Read Daniel 8:15-26, Daniel 9:20-27.

Compare the overshadowing in Exodus 40:34-36, Exodus 24:15-16, Luke 1:35, and Luke 9:35.

Compare the promises of mercy to Adam (Gen 3:15), Abraham (Gen 22:18), David (2 Sam 7:12) & Luke 1:50.

John the Baptist is Born
3rd Sunday of Advent
Luke 1:57-80

Catechism references to Luke 1:57-80
422: God has visited His people
706: Spirit of promise   523: St. John the Baptist
717: Precursor, prophet, baptist

     Genesis 17:10-14 and Leviticus 12:3 provide us with the Hebrew rules on circumcision. Once the male child was circumcised, that child was responsible for keeping the whole law of Moses, all the food regulations, the clothing regulations, the regulations on washing, sacrifices, offerings – everything. Acts 15:1-29 shows Peter describing what a burden circumcision and the law of Moses placed on the Hebrews. Paul tells the Galatians this as well, in Galatians 5:2-6 and Galatians 6:12-16. But in Colossians 2:11-13, Paul makes an interesting connection. He says that circumcision and baptism are linked, and in Romans 6:4, Paul explicitly links baptism with the crucifixion. Putting all these references together, we see that God gave circumcision to the Hebrews in order to show them how impossible it is for man to save himself. At the same time, circumcision "on the eighth day" foreshadows the work of Christ on the Cross. Because the Sabbath day was called the seventh day, for on this day God rested and because Jesus rose on Sunday, Christians have long associated the number "eight" with the sacrament of baptism and with salvation itself. God shows that what is impossible for men is possible for God. The Old Testament ritual surrounding circumcision is God's hint to us of what the Cross would mean and what it would accomplish.

     In a certain sense, Zechariah's unwillingness to believe the angel is linked to the Apostle Thomas' unwillingness to believe that Jesus is truly risen from the dead (John 20:24-29). Zechariah is engaging in the marital act with his wife, but doesn't believe that God actually has the power to make the act bring forth new life. Thomas watched Jesus raise Lazarus from the dead - in fact, it is Thomas who exhorts the apostles to accompany Jesus to Lazarus' tomb (John 11:16) – yet he is unable to believe that Jesus can himself be raised to new life (John 20:24-29). Thus, Luke's story hear is directly linked to what Luke tells us about both the Resurrection and Pentecost. When the angel first came to Zechariah, fear fell upon him (Luke 1:12). After Zechariah regains the ability to speak, fear fell upon all of his neighbors (Luke 1:65). When the apostles first see the risen Christ, fear falls upon them (Luke 24:37), when they speak at Pentecost, those who listen are cut to the heart (Acts 2:37). In Zechariah's confirmation that his son's name will be John, which means "God is gracious", God is telling us that we will see more of his grace being poured out, if only we pay attention to events.

Malachi 4:5 prophecies the coming of the one who is identified in Luke 1:76, and Luke 7:26 specifically makes the connection between the prophecy and the fulfillment. Similarly, Isaiah 9:2 and Luke 1:79 are very closely linked passages, Isaiah prophesying what Luke fulfills. Thus, Zechariah's words, as quoted by Luke, together demonstrate that the whole Old Testament has been pointing to the events which are even now happening as Zechariah speaks. Like Mary's Magnificat, which is prayed by all religious every morning in the prayer called "The Liturgy of the Hours," Zechariah's canticle (verses 68-79), is called the Benedictus, and is prayed every morning by everyone under religious vows and many lay Catholics. Together, morning prayer, with the Benedictus at its center, and evening prayer, with the Magnificat at its center, are called the "hinge prayers", the prayers upon which all other prayers of the Liturgy of the Hours depend.

Notice the similarities and differences between the two canticles. While in the Benedictus Zechariah's words bless God, in the Magnificat Mary's very being blesses God (verses 46, 68), while the Benedictus proclaims salvation open to the Hebrews, the Magnificat speaks not only of the salvation of the Hebrews, but of the whole of humanity (verses 50, 70-73), while the Benedictus shows a father blessing his son, in the Magnificat, Mary pronounces blessings on herself (verses 48, 76-78). The Magnificat is at once more universal and much more personal than the Benedictus is, directed at both Mary specifically and the whole of humanity in the way that the Benedictus is not. This is why the Benedictus is the morning prayer – it reminds us of the morning of God's covenant, the beginnings of the Old Testament, while the Magnificat's evening prayer tells us of the full scope of salvation, brought to us through the Virgin's womb.

This is why Luke 1:80 is such an excellent closing verse for the Benedictus. Because the Benedictus is a summary of the whole of the Old Testament and a testimony of the imminent fulfillment of everything the Old Testament pointed towards, John is likewise a living example of this imminent fulfillment. Just as the Israelites lived in the wilderness prior to being taken into the Promised Land, so John lives in the wilderness prior to the time of his work. While in the desert, God cleansed the Israelites of their idols, and John "grew and became strong in spirit." The life of the nation of Israel in the desert, the life of John in the desert, both of these are examples of how we as Christians are called to the desert, to difficulties, dry times, work, formation, study, prayer. The nation of Israel and the person we know as John the Baptist are examples to us. We as Christians are called to proclaim the way of the Lord and make straight his path. If we do this work well, then we gain what the Israelites gained in the Promised Land, what John gained in his martyrdom – we gain heaven itself.

Jesus is Born
4th Sunday of Advent
Luke 2:1-20

Catechism reference to Luke 2:1-20

333: Song of the angels   525: The Christmas Mystery
437: Christ   559: Jesus enters Jerusalem
448: Lord   695: Anointing and the Spirit
486:Conceived by Spirit   725: Communion with Christ
515:Mystery of Christ   2599: Jesus prays

Luke promised us an orderly account of the events of everything that has happened, and so far he has kept his word. First, he described the annunciation of John, then the annunciation of Jesus, the birth and circumcision of John, now the birth and circumcision of Jesus. Luke's careful attention to detail and his incorporation of eyewitness testimony is further attested to by his description of the census. As is so often the case, the account of the census actually serves a two-fold purpose. First, since it is a real historical event, it helps us locate the event of the Incarnation in human history, but second, and more important, it is a sign of the work God intends to accomplish among men, "a decree went out from Caesar Augustus that the whole world should be enrolled." This is exactly what the King of Kings intended through His Incarnation – to enroll the entire world into the Kingdom of God, which is the Church. What Caesar Augustus attempts to do in a limited and human fashion, God himself will begin to establish through His grace. When this passage is read in conjunction with John 3:17, the stark contrast between human and divine work is made clear.

Luke continues throughout his narrative to record details that are important both for their historical accuracy and also for the deeper spiritual meaning contained within them. For instance, he emphasizes that Jesus was laid in a manger, mentioning it three different times within less than ten verses (Luke 2:7, 12, 16). A manger is an eating trough for animals. When we read John 6:54-56, we see this simple detail really has a deeper meaning. The word "Beth-le-hem" means "House of Bread." So,

Luke tells us that God took on flesh in the House of Bread and was laid in an eating trough.

What he says here actually fulfills several prophetic historical events from the Old Testament. After the spirit of God moved over the waters, Adam and Eve were created in the Garden of Eden. They were given the right to eat of the fruit of the trees, including the fruit of the tree of life (Genesis 2:16-17). In other words, Adam and Eve, along with the whole of creation, were in a sense baptized into existence and given the ability to eat of the fruit of the tree of life. When they ate the fruit of the tree of the knowledge of good and evil, they committed a deadly sin. Adam and Eve were kicked out not just for this sin, but in order to keep them from eating of the tree of life (Genesis 3:22-23). Why is this important? Recall that Jesus was hung on a tree (1 Peter 2:24). What hangs from a tree is the fruit of the tree, and the tree of the cross is the source of our life in God. Thus, the cross is the tree of life, and Jesus' flesh is its fruit. Genesis 1 through 3 foreshadow baptism and Eucharist.

The foreshadowing of baptism and Eucharist can be found throughout the Old Testament. When Noah was saved through the waters along with his family, eight persons in all (there's that "eight" number again), through the wood of the ark (representing the wood of the Cross), God permitted them to eat flesh and gave to them the same command to be fruitful and multiply that had been given to Adam. As 1 Peter 3:20-21 reminds us, Noah's salvation prefigures baptism. Noah and his family could eat flesh after the Flood because they were "baptized" through the Flood, saved from a sinful world. What happened to them corresponds to our ability to partake of the Eucharist after we have been baptized and our slavery to sin has been broken. Thus it is not surprising to remember that when Moses lead his people through the waters of the Red Sea, and their slavery to the Egyptians was broken, they were given bread from heaven – manna – to eat (Exodus 16:4). Jesus will specifically make this link between manna and His own flesh in John 6. Luke makes this link later in chapter 2, tying together circumcision (another foreshadowing of baptism as we saw last week) and Eucharist.

The angels announce Jesus' birth to the shepherds, inviting them to celebrate the birth of the Savior. The first king over

Israel, Saul, was called a shepherd by God (2 Sam 5:2) and Ezekiel 34:23-24 likewise shows that David was a shepherd to his people. For the Israelites, royalty were called "shepherds" because they led people as a shepherd leads his flock. When we read 1 Peter 2:9, we recall that our baptism makes us a holy nation, a royal priesthood, a people set apart. Because Jesus Christ is priest, prophet and king, our baptism into Jesus transforms each of us into priest, prophet and king. That is, *we* are kings in part because we lead others to Jesus Christ. Thus, the appearance of Jesus to the shepherds at the Incarnation prefigures the royal kingship God bestowed on us through His second appearance to us at the Resurrection. Indeed, Jesus Himself confirmed our kingship by greeting the first women he saw after the Resurrection with the royal greeting "Chairoo!" which means "Hail!" – the same greeting the angel used to Mary at the Incarnation (see week two). The summoning of the shepherds to the manger fore-shadows the royal transformation accomplished in us when we are baptized and go to dine at the Mass, the Lamb's Feast. When we read Heb 1:6 in conjunction with this passage in Luke, we suddenly become aware of the myriads of angels present at Mass, kneeling at the consecration with us.

The angels sing glory and praise to God in Luke 2:14, then the shepherds approach the manger, worship and go out into the world, proclaiming what has happened (Luke 2:17-20). We often forget that Luke 2:14 is the basis for the Gloria that is sung in Mass. If we study the Mass, we will see exactly the same order of events: we sing the Gloria, the Eucharist is consecrated, and we all go forward to worship, to take and eat. If we faith-fully followed the example of Mary and the shepherds, we would receive the Eucharist, meditate, pray and ponder on it as Mary did, then go out into the world. Indeed, the very word "Mass" comes from the Latin "ite misse," which means "You are sent." The Mass is intended to remind us of not only of His death, but of the Incarnation.

The centrality of the Incarnation to the Mass and the life of the Church explains a rather peculiar thing observant visitors to a Catholic Church notice. Every Sunday during the recitation of the Nicene Creed, the whole congregation bows while pray-ing the lines: "By the power of the Holy Spirit, He was born of the Virgin Mary and became man." However, on two days of the year, the Feast of the Annunciation and Christmas Day, the whole congregation kneels during those two lines instead of simply bowing. We kneel on those two days because we remind ourselves of the moment God took on flesh at the Annunciation and the moment God's enfleshment became known to the whole world, Christmas Day.

Thus, Luke 2 tells us that the prophecy concerning Bethlehem that can be found in Micah 5:2 is fulfilled. Because it is fulfilled, the prophecy of Psalm 110:1-2 will likewise be fulfilled. As we have seen so far, literally dozens of prophecies are coming to their fullness. More is still to come.

Jesus and Mary are Purified
Christmas Sunday
Luke 2:21-40

Catechism **references to Luke 2:21-40**
149: Mary's belief
587: The Stumbling Block
527: Jesus' circumcision
618: Participating in Jesus' sacrifice
529: Presentation in the Temple
695: Anointing and the Spirit
575: Sign of Contradiction
711: The Remnant
583: Jesus and the Temple
713: The Messiah's characteristics

Leviticus 12:2-8 describes the consequences of giving birth, ritual impurity, and how the woman is to cleanse herself and her child. The Hebrew idea of impurity is rather confusing to the modern mind, because it applies both to that which is holy and that which is unholy. For instance, touching a corpse causes defilement, but touching the sacred scrolls of the Torah likewise "soils the hands." How can this be? The reason is straightforward. When we approach the sacred, we are made conscious of our own sinfulness. Coming in contact with the sacred brings to us who are sinners the desire to be pure as the sacred is pure. As we know from Leviticus 17:11-14, blood is sacred because it is the source of life. Thus, when someone touches or is touched by blood, they are in contact with the sacred. This is why everyone who came in contact with blood, such as a woman giving birth to a child, was required to cleanse themselves – the contact with such a sacred thing, especially in such a sacred event, would properly evoke in the persons involved a desire to be pure.

Some Christians point to this passage to justify their opinion that Mary was a sinner in need of purification, but the context does not support the concept. We must remember that Jesus is also circumcised in this passage, even though He has no need of circumcision in order to be joined to the family of God

– He is already of the family of God, being the Son of God. Matthew 3:15 provides the interpretive key. As Matthew tells us, Jesus is baptized in order to fulfill all righteousness, that is, in order to avoid scandalizing people who do not fully understand who He is. Similarly, His circumcision and Mary's purification are also ways by which God begins to introduce Himself and His mother to the Chosen People, His family. Though both are already pure, Mary living her life without sin and Jesus being God, they both come forward because this is God's command for all of Israel; Mary is a daughter of Israel, Jesus is a son.

However, there is a further reason to come forward. In offering Jesus to God at the Temple, Mary prefigures the work of the Cross. The smallest drop of the blood of Christ is sufficient to pay for all the sins of men, past, present and future. Here at the circumcision, Christ begins the spilling of His blood. Though the payment has begun, God wants to fully reveal Himself to us, He desires to superabundantly pay for our sins. Just as Mary willingly allows her Son to offer Himself on the Cross, so Mary willingly begins this offering of her Son to the Father here, in the Temple.

The name "Jesus" means "Yahweh saves." He receives it now, on the eighth day after his birth because God will complete the work of our justification thirty three years later on another eighth day, Easter Sunday. "Simeon" whose name means "God has heard," has prayed his whole life that he might live to witness the beginning of the redemption of man. God honors his prayers, and enlightens his mind, so that he can recognize the Messiah he has sought for so long.

Simeon's appearance is important for other reasons, however. The Liturgy of the Hours contains yet a third prayer, Simeon's prayer of thanksgiving in Luke 2:29-32. This canticle is called the Nunc Dimittis; it is prayed by every person under religious vows every night immediately before bed. Since many lay Catholics also pray the Liturgy of the Hours, they also pray the Nunc Dimittis before bed. Praying the Liturgy of the Hours involves praying through many different Psalms and Scripture readings on a rotating schedule, but these three prayers, Mary's Magnificat, Zechariah's Benedictus, and Simeon's Nunc Dimittis, are the only three Scripture passages which are prayed every day without fail. Notice that, like Mary's prayer, Simeon proclaims the salvation which is made available to all peoples everywhere. Further, his canticle unites the themes found in both Mary's and Zecheriah's canticles, for he proclaims that Jesus is a light for revelation to the Gentiles and for glory to God's people, Israel."

The Church has an ancient saying, *lex orandi, lex credendi* – "as we pray, so we believe." Given the centrality of the Liturgy of the Hours to the life of the Church, the fact that the three major prayers of this liturgy are all drawn from Luke's infancy narrative demonstrates the absolute centrality of the Incarnation to our salvation. Because God took on human flesh, all humanity is joined to God. Thus, even though many Jews of Jesus' time thought prophecy was dead, Simeon and Anna demonstrate that this idea was incorrect (Luke 2:29-38). Their canticles of prophecy accurately demonstrated what would, in fact, happen to the world as a result of the Incarnation.

The centrality of the Incarnation itself points to the centrality of Mary's role in our salvation. In Hebrews 4:12 and Luke 2:34-35, we see Scripture drawing a very interesting parallel between itself and Mary. Scripture often refers to Mary holding and contemplating her Son and the events surrounding Him in her heart. Simeon's canticle is echoed by Paul in Hebrews, but where Simeon speaks of Mary, Paul speaks of Scripture. Scripture tells us that both Mary and the Word of God accomplish similar work on our hearts – through contemplation of either, our thoughts are revealed.

This need for prayer and contemplation is re-affirmed by the example of Anna, an eighty-four year old widow who fasted and prayed before God in the Temple every day. This spiritual preparation allowed her to recognize the Saviour. Without this preparation, would she have been able to recognize Him? It seems unlikely. Jesus lived out a model life for us, demonstrating to everyone how we are to live in order to walk in God's ways. He constantly undertook fasting and prayer, constantly keeping His human flesh in obedience to His human and divine wills.

Fasting has great results, whether the fast be from food, drink, television, football, or something else, and whether the fast be five minutes or several days. Fasting teaches us how to control our passing impulses to do this or that, it establishes patience in us, and the lack which we feel when we deliberately deny our impulses to do something we like can build up in us a hunger for the presence of God. We don't have to fast from food — fasting from activities we like can build up that same hunger for God. We don't have to fast for days — a refusal to take a drink for just five minutes when we are thirsty, or a refusal to take seconds at dinner, even these small refusals to give into the impulses of our flesh can have tremendous merit, as long as we consciously join these small offerings to the perfect offering of Jesus Christ on the Cross.

Wise Men/Slaughter of the Innocents
Commemorated on the Feasts of the Epiphany and the Slaughter of the Innocents, Dec 28
Matthew 2:1-23

***Catechism* references to Matthew 2:1-23**
333: The Song of the Angels
439: Son of David
486: The Christ in Mary's womb
528: The Epiphany
530: The flight into Egypt
724: Mary manifests the Son

In Micah 5:1-3, Micah prophesies the coming of the Messiah from the town of Bethlehem. Ruth, one of Jesus Gentile ancestors, came to live in Bethlehem, according to Ruth 1:1-19 and Matthew 1:5, Jesse, one of his Jewish ancestors, was from Bethlehem according to 1 Sam 17:12 and Matthew 1:6, and David was likewise both born in Bethlehem and crowned in Bethlehem according to 1 Sam 16. The "House of Bread" which is Bethlehem thus combines both Gentiles and Jews into one people. In this way, God prefigures how the Eucharist will join all men into one people, His Family.

The Gentiles are represented not only in the connections to Bethlehem, but also in the wise men who come seeking the Saviour. When God takes away the star from the wise men's sight, they ask for direction from a secular authority, King Herod. God established the Church precisely in order to guide us when we are confused or lose our way. Our "guiding lights", whether they be people or habits we rely on, can fail us, but the Church cannot. Her teachings are an unfailing guide to do what is right. This kind of unfailing guidance is prefigured in the way God touches the lives of the wise men through a dream – when they hear this warning, they change their plans. The warnings of the Church about certain habits of thought or ways of living life are likewise meant to turn us away from danger. Just as the wise men's decision to change their plans saved Jesus' life, so our decisions to change our plans because of what the Church tells us can save our lives and the lives of others.

When we read Psalm 72:10-15, Isaiah 49:7, or Isaiah 60:6,10-13, we see how the words of God's prophets concerning the Gentiles are fulfilled here in the infancy narratives. Gold represents kingship, incense represents the offering made to God, and myrrh represents suffering. In each of these gifts, and in their sum together, we find an example of how God continually foreshadows what He is about to do. While we don't normally think of the Incarnation this way, even at infancy, when the Son of God took the form of a slave, the beginning of the Passion of Christ can be found. The depths to which God humbled Himself in simply taking on human flesh are demonstrated to us by these gifts. The infinite God who transcends time and space chose to limit Himself by taking on human flesh and occupying a specific time, a specific place.

In Acts 14:16-17, Luke reminds us of the many ways in which God gives signs of His presence to us. Paul does the same in Romans 2:14-15. While Jewish shepherds were told of Jesus' birth by an angel and Simeon and Anna were told by the Holy Spirit, that is, by direct revelation from God, the Gentile Magi were informed of Jesus by a star, that is, by the evidence of the natural world. Indeed, even Old Testament Scriptures, such as Wisdom 13:1-9, remind us that the very existence of the universe a testimony to God. Though the Gentiles who are the Magi do not know Scripture, still, careful study brought them to Jesus. The superstition of astrology is broken by the star of Bethlehem, for through this star, the Magi come to know the God who made the stars, the heavens and the earth and all that is in them. Though someone can ask us how we know God exists, and we can answer simply by pointing to the natural world around us, still, we must realize that this is a very difficult way to learn about God. Of all the Gentiles, only the Magi were able to discern what was happening. The Jews, who had the advantage of the Scriptures through which God reveals Himself to us, were much more prepared for the Saviour.

Thus, it is the Jews, not the Gentiles, who are asked to be martyrs for the infant Jesus. Thomas Aquinas and Augustine together say the Holy Innocents suffered as martyrs and confessed Christ not by speaking but by dying. The children saved themselves for heaven through this event as surely as Baptism saves children today. The feast of the Holy Innocents is December 28th. This is an important concept to keep in mind even today, for as Jeremiah 31:15 reminds us, innocent children who witness Christ simply by their existence and who are killed simply because they exist are easily found today.

The call to turn towards Christ is constant, and catches us in our daily work. Scripture shows us that it has always been so. God called Moses while shepherding (Ex 3:1), Elisha while ploughing (1 Kings 19:19-20), Amos as he looked after his herd (Amos 7:15), and the wise men as they worked.

God intends our work to have meaning. Though Hosea prophesied that God would call His Son out of Egypt, Hosea 11:1 does not say how this would occur. Joseph is not scandalized by a God who won't save Himself. Instead, Joseph does the work of a father, taking his family to Egypt without asking when he will be able to return. Likewise, upon returning, God confirms his suspicions about the safety of Judea. Though Mary is the greatest of saints, God sets Joseph up as the guardian and guide of both Mary and God. God has always relied on our cooperation in order to accomplish His purpose. He placed His life on earth in the hands of His parents, Mary and Joseph. Though Joseph was not a biological parent, still, his care for Jesus made him a true parent. God did not set Joseph up as an empty figurehead, nor does He set any one of us up to be such a thing. He intends us to expend real energy, dig into the work He has given, and make it our own through our efforts and His assistance. In this way, we show ourselves to be true children of the living God.

The Finding in the Temple
Luke 2:41-52

Catechism references to Luke 2:41-52

472: Christ' human knowledge   534: Finding Jesus in the Temple
503: Sign of Mary's Virginity   583: Jesus and the Temple
517: Christ's life/redemption   2196: The First Commandment
531: Jesus' hidden life   2599: Jesus prays

The Hebrew word "to hear" also means "to obey." According to Hebrews 5:8, obedience is the only thing God learned on earth, and he learned it through suffering. He learned in the sense that He constantly chose to experience in His own human flesh the eternal obedience to the Father He already possessed from eternity. Though Jesus gives the appearance of disobedience to Mary and Joseph here, He is really being obedient. This paradox recalls to us another paradox which will be raised for us at the end of the Gospels: the Cross appears to be the sign of failure, as all the apostles scatter rather than face it, but it ends up being the source of triumph. In the same way, Jesus' obedience to the will of the Father is not a failure to obey Joseph or Mary. Jesus does the Father's will by teaching in the Temple. His parents want Him to obey God. The moment Joseph and Mary express what they want Him to do, He does so.

So, when we read Luke's account of Jesus growing in wisdom and strength, we must remember that Luke is referring to two things: first, he is referring to the way in which Jesus' human flesh grew in strength, the way in which Jesus' human intellect grew in its ability to grasp and hold onto the things which Jesus already knew in His divine intellect, and the way in which Jesus' human will grew in its own power. Second, through his phrasing, Luke intends to remind us of one of the greatest of the Old Testament prophets. When we compare Luke 2:40 and Luke 2:52 with 1 Sam 2:26 and 1 Sam 3:1-10, we see that Luke intended his readers to read his verses and remember what they saw in 1 Samuel. In 1 Samuel 16:1-13, Samuel will anoint a hidden king in Bethlehem, the House of Bread, and will die after that king is greatly persecuted and faces death (1 Sam 25:1). In this way, we see that Samuel's life was a foreshadowing of the life of the Son of God in the flesh. Here in the infancy narratives, we likewise see the hidden King of kings, who will be anointed by the Holy Spirit at baptism, and who will be greatly persecuted, even unto death itself.

This passage in Luke is meant to be a foreshadowing of the entire Gospel, especially the Crucifixion. It is here that Jesus for the first time declares himself the son of the Father. It is also the last time Luke will call the interpreters of the Mosaic law and traditions "teachers." From now on, Jesus alone will carry that title. The mantle has been lifted from the shoulders of the rabbis and priests God established among His Chosen People and is now passed to His only-begotten Son. Jesus will, in turn, pass this title and all of its authority on to the Apostles He chooses, when He tells them in John 20:21, "Even as I was sent, so I send you."

Because God establishes everything that happens in the world, because it is at the Temple that the title "Teacher" moves to Jesus, and because Jesus was most perfectly Teacher on the Cross, all of the events surrounding this most important event will in some way echo the events of the Crucifixion. As the Holy Family's journey up to Jerusalem for the Passover, they foreshadow Christ's journey with his apostles up to Jerusalem immediately prior to his death (Luke 19:27). Mary and Joseph search for three days, reminding us of the three days of loss Mary will suffer after the crucifixion parallel Mary's loss after the crucifixion, fulfilling the prophecy of John 2:20-21. When we read 1 Peter 4:6 and its description of Jesus preaching in the spirit to the dead in prison, we recall that Jesus preached first in the flesh to the rabbis in the Temple, men He would later call "white-washed tombs" (Matthew 23:27). Mary's pondering of these things in her heart in Luke 2:52 foreshadows the Church's contemplation of Jesus after the Resurrection, as the apostles, the heart of the Church, hid in a locked upper room. Even now in the Temple, Simeon's prediction concerning the sword of sorrow that would pierce Mary's heart is coming true. This loss begins the preparation for a much greater loss later on.

If we carefully study the Gospel of Luke, we will discover a remarkable thing: The story Luke tells begins in the Temple in Luke 1:8-9 and it ends in the Temple, in Luke 24:53. The finding in the Temple is not just a pleasant story Luke threw in, it is a compact summary of everything he wants to tell us about Jesus, a kind of Gospel within the Gospel.

When we consider that every event and every silence in the Gospel is meant to bring us to a deeper understanding of God and how He works in our lives, the long gap in both Matthew and Luke between the infancy narratives and the adult ministry Jesus undertakes is a sign to us. By allowing this silence to work in our hearts, we begin to understand that Jesus' "hidden life," the life he lives from the age of about twelve to perhaps His thirtieth year, is a sharing in, an experience of, the ordinary hidden life of men and women throughout the world. Every day, several billion people get up, live out the day's events in small villages and towns throughout the world, and lay down again to that little foreshadowing of death which is sleep. Every night and every morning, we are one step closer to the death that awaits us all. When death comes to find us, we will pass through its doorway and meet God face to face, the God who knew from before the moment of His conception what death was, and how He would deal with it. This silence is the last thing we can take from the infancy narratives, the last gift we can carry forward into the adult life through which the Gospel is made fully known.

CONCLUSION

The first Christians said "God writes the world like men write words." God author not only the words of the Gospel, but also the events which inspired the words. Like a historical play or novel, in which the events both really happened and serve to give us moral insights on how we are to live, the whole of Scripture is an enormous morality play. It is records truly historical events, which "happened to them as a warning, but they were written down for our instruction, upon whom the end of the ages has come" (1 Cor 10:11). God has not finished writing this world. God's plan is not a past, finished event. It is a dynamic, living reality in which we each have a role to play. With every wailing newborn child, we are presented with an image of God who does not yet know God, who is lost in a world broken by sin. Each child must be led to the waters of baptism, washed and transformed into a true son or daughter, and taught the fullness of the new heritage born within through grace. Once we have been transformed, we must know the story of our God, and thereby our own story. The Church is our heritage, our mother, our family, the Bride who makes us her children, true children of God, and Scripture is our dowry, the wealth that tells us who we are.

Daily
Scripture Study

John the Baptist is Announced
1st week of Advent covers Luke 1:1-25
Session 1 – READ Luke 1:1-4

Scripture references and Themes
1-4 – Revelation - Acts 1:1-5, 21-22; 1 Cor 15:3, Heb 3:1, 1
John 1:1, John 15:27, 20:31, Lk 24:48

In Luke 1:1-4, we see Luke laying the foundation for his
Gospel account, an account which actually has two parts. Luke
wrote both the Gospel named for him and the Acts of the
Apostles, intending the two to be read together as one story.
Indeed, if you compare Luke 1:1-4 with Acts 1:1-5, Luke him-
self tells us this.

Luke's opening Gospel passage tells us several things. First,
we discover that many people who were not eyewitnesses, including Luke, are compiling accounts of the life of Jesus. Second, these accounts are based on the testimony of still-living
eyewitnesses. Third, Luke is writing "an orderly account" to
Theophilus. A fourth useful piece of information is that
"Theophilus" literally means in Greek "One who loves God."
So, what can we take away from the first four verses of the
Gospel of Luke? We know that this Gospel is based on eyewitness accounts, we know that God intends this Gospel account
to be orderly, so that we may better comprehend it, and we
know that it is addressed to the one who loves God. That is, in
a very real sense, God is speaking to each one of us here, establishing his credentials with us, demonstrating his love and the
care that He takes in order to make sure that we will have a very
clear idea about Him and His relationship to us.

The first thing a careful reader will be struck by are the
details Luke supplies. He tells us the words of the conversation
between the angel and Zechariah while they were together in the
temple as Zechariah burned incense. During this time, Zechariah
was alone with the angel. This means Luke had to have interviewed Zechariah to find out the particulars of the story. Likewise, the conversation he records between Mary and the archan-
gel Gabriel was an intimate conversation, known only to those

two. Mary must have related these details to Luke, for no one else would have known them. Indeed, many Scripture scholars have noted that the first two chapters of Luke are written in a Greek that is stylistically quite different from the rest of the Gospel. The first two chapters actually appear to be a translation from another language into Greek. This is not surprising when we remember that Mary and Zechariah undoubtedly spoke Aramaic as their first language. Luke is giving us their accounts in their own words, translating their Aramaic directly into the Greek.

Luke's insistence on using eyewitness accounts is characteristic of apostolic preaching. Paul, for instance, tells us this. The Gospel the apostles all preach is the Gospel each one of them heard himself from the Lord (1 Cor 15:3, Heb 3:1). John's first letter will likewise begin with the same assertion – the apostles preach only what they have seen with their own eyes and touched with their own hands (1 John 1:1). When the office of apostle is empty, Peter insists it can only be filled by someone who has been a physical witness to the fact of Jesus Christ (Acts 1:21-22). The apostles stick strictly to the facts – what they can personally testify to - so that everyone may come to belief and have eternal life (John 20:31). At the Last Supper, Jesus told the apostles to act as His witnesses, and He repeated the command again after His Resurrection (Jn 15:27, Luke 24:48). The Gospel writers, like the other apostles, are faithful to His commands.

Questions for study:
1. What does Luke promise about his rendition of events?
2. What evidence seems to indicate he really has interviewed eyewitnesses?
3. Is his insistence on eyewitness accounts unusual? How do we know?
4. What do these answers tell us about the way God reveals Himself to us?
5. How could this information be useful when we talk to other people about Jesus?

John the Baptist is Announced
1st week of Advent covers Luke 1:1-25
Session 2 – READ Luke 1:5-7

Scripture references and Themes
1:5 – Time, priestly divisions - Mt 2:1, 1 Chron 24:10, 2 Chron 31:2
1:7 – Barrenness - Gen 15:3, 16:1, 18:11, 25:21, 29:31, 30:1, 30:24, Jgs 13:2-5, 1 Sam 1:2-6

Both Matthew and Luke agree on the time and place of Jesus' birth: it occurred during Herod's reign in Judea. Today, some people refuse to believe the Gospel accounts because the four accounts of Jesus' life sometimes differ with one another in certain details. However, disagreements between the four accounts is not fatal to the truth of the Gospel. We must remember that first-century Jews told stories in a markedly different way than 20th-century readers are accustomed to. We are used to strict chronology – if A, B and C happened in a certain order, then they must be told in that order. For them, however, if A and C shared a common theme or served to illustrate a point, it was perfectly reasonable to group A and C together and leave B to be told at a later time. The writer would not tell the reader that events had been "grouped by theme." Jewish Scripture has always relied heavily on oral teaching traditions. Teachers were expected to guide students through the readings. The writer assumed every reader had a teacher who would orally explain the proper order of events if the need arose.

Today's three verses carry two interesting themes. The first concerns Zechariah and Elizabeth. Both Zechariah and Elizabeth hold privileged positions in the nation of Israel: Elizabeth descends from Aaron, Moses' brother (Exodus 4:27). Aaron performed the first four miracles in front of Pharoah and was the first high priest, anointed by Moses himself. Zechariah, as a male descendant of Aaron, is therefore also a Levitical priest. As Matthew 1:7 shows, Abijah, Zechariah's forefather, is the great-grandson of David and also a forefather of Jesus. Abijah's family had obtained, through lot, the eighth place in the service of the Temple, a fact whose significance will be explored in the next session. Yet, though the lineage of both Zechariah and Elizabeth are noble, Luke follows by telling us something even more important: both Elizabeth and Zechariah were righteous and blameless. What Luke says about them reminds us of what the apostle Paul will tell us about himself in 1 Corinthians 4:3-5 and Phillippians 3:4-6.

However, neither their righteousness nor their nobility protects them from sterility. The two results of the Fall were greatly multiplied pain in childbearing for the woman and increased toil for the man in securing food (Gen 3:16-19). The first three patriarchs, Abraham, Isaac, and Jacob, each experienced a severe famine which required them to leave their homes. Each of their wives experienced the greatest pain of childbearing, sterility. Hannah, the woman who brought forth the first prophet to ever anoint a king over Israel, was sterile, as was the woman who brought forth Samson, the strength of Israel. Elizabeth's patiently borne sterility, healed by God, results in the greatest prophet of Scripture, John the Baptist. In each healing, God shows forth His power to heal the consequences of our sins.

Questions for study:
1.   God's Chosen People relied on oral tradition to understand Scripture. How does this understanding correspond to Catholic teaching?
2.   Zechariah and Elizabeth were of exalted lineage, but they also lived holy lives. We are made priest, prophet and king by baptism. How does Luke show us that Zechariah and Elizabeth are models for baptized people?
3.   God permitted each of the sterile women in Scripture to bear important children. How are these women an example to us that every child is always a gift from God?
4.   God is Life. Human life is a gift from God. How does the use of temporary or permanent self-sterilization affect our relationship with God?

John the Baptist is Announced
1st week of Advent covers Luke 1:1-25
Session 3 – READ Luke 1:8-12

Catechism references to Luke 1:11
332: The work of angels in the divine plan

Scripture references and Themes
1:9 – Burning incense - Ex 30:7
1:11 – Angelic appearances - Lk 2:9, Acts 5:19

Zechariah's family was chosen by lot to be the eighth priestly family. Zechariah was chosen by lot to burn incense. This ancient Hebrew tradition of casting lots to determine function and office in divine liturgy will be seen again in Acts 1:26, when it is used to choose between Matthias and Barsabbas to fill the office of apostle. As Num 26:55, 33:54 or Judges 20:9 shows us, the casting of lots was a divinely instituted method for choosing successors or dividing up property. In fact, these Old Testament passages show us that the use of lot was the key to inheritance. When the Promised Land was divided up among the Twelve tribes, it was divided by lot. Thus, Zechariah's being chosen by lot for the Temple worship is a sign that a new inheritance is coming.

Zechariah was the priest chosen to burn incense in the Temple. The burning of incense before the presence of God began with the Ark of the Covenant (Ex 30:1), continued through the priestly service in the Temple, and was seen by the apostle John in the vision he recorded, the Book of Revelation (Rev 5:8, 8:3-4). The burning of incense is still performed today. The incense represents both the prayers of the faithful rising to God and the sweet odor of the perfect sacrifice the Son of God made on the Cross.

The Jews burned incense for two reasons, one of which they realized, and a second they did not. They knew the smoke of incense represented the prayers of all the faithful, rising up to God as a pleasing aroma before Him. This is why the whole people prayed outside the temple at the hour of incense – the actions within were actively linked with the actions outside. What they did not realize was that the thurimer (or censor), in which the incense burned, was itself a symbol of the Incarnation God was about to accomplish. The censor in which the burning coal is contained represents Jesus' human nature, the burning coals inside it represent the divine nature of God, who is a consuming fire (Hebrews 12:29). Thus, when Christians use the censor we are reminded that all of our prayers rise to God only God in the flesh. Only through Jesus Christ, the one mediator between God and man (1 Timothy 2:5) are our prayers made effective. This is why it is most appropriate to use the censor during Mass and Eucharistic benediction. It unites our understanding as the prayers and the incense were united at the Temple. The incense and the thurimer are symbolic representations of God Incarnate, Christ and His mediation. God comes to dwell among us in answer to the prayers of His People.

This Eucharistic connection, God coming in the flesh, is foreshadowed in two additional ways. First, Zechariah's family was the eighth of the 24 groups of Levitical priests (1 Chronicles 24:7-19). Jesus, the first Apostle and our High Priest (Hebrews 3:1), rose one day after the seventh (sabbath) day, that is, He rose on the eighth day (Sunday). Zechariah's eighth-group priesthood is thus symbolically linked to the eighth-day Resurrection. Second, the angel appeared silently to Zechariah near the altar, the place of sacrifice. Only priests offer sacrifice. From that location, Gabriel announced God's preparations for the coming of the True High Priest.

John will be made exceptionally holy and will lead many to salvation. His whole life prepares the Messiah's way. "John" means "God is gracious." As Paul reminds us in 1 Cor 3:9, we are God's co-workers. Through the prophets of the Old Testament and through Zechariah and John the Baptist, God graciously allows men to prepare His way. In Luke 7:26-27, he will remind us that Jesus Himself links the prophecy of Malachi 3:1 to John's coming.

Here, Zecheriah is struck by fear at the presence of an angel. At Jesus' birth, the shepherds will react the same way. When Peter is in prison, he is so struck by the angelic presence that he thinks he is having a vision. Angels are messengers of God, sent to help men know how best to do God's will. They are living signs of communion with God. Their presence is strongest in the infancy narratives and the Resurrection accounts.

Questions for study:
1. What does a censor symbolize? What does incense symbolize?
2. Why is it appropriate to use incense in the celebration of the Mass?
3. In the first century, sons took the vocations of their fathers. Why doesn't John do this? What could be more important than offering sacrifice to God as a Levitical priest?
4. An altar is a place of sacrifice. Read Mt 14:8-10. How is John's whole life, even from the moment of the angel's announcement, a foreshadowing of Christ?
5. How does the *Catechism's* description improve your understanding of angels?

John the Baptist is Announced
1st week of Advent covers Luke 1:1-25
Session 4 – READ Luke 1:13-16

Catechism **references to Luke 1:15-19**
717: A man sent by God

Scripture References and Themes
1:13 – Name-giving - Gen 2:19-20, Lk 1:30, 57, 60, 63, Mt
1:20-21, 1 Cor 3:9, 1 Cor 4:15
1:15 – Nazirite vow - Num 6:3, Lk 7:33, Jgs 13:4, 1 Sam 1:11
(LXX)

Giving a name demonstrates authority and stewardship.
Scripture shows Adam's authority over the animals by the fact
that he was permitted to name them. Similarly, though God
provides the names for both John the Baptist and Jesus, the act
of naming is left to the parents. God intends us to be His co-
workers (1 Cor 3:9). He gives every person real authority in the
world. This is especially true of parents, for every bringing forth
of a child is a vibrant share in the work of creation. We are
parents biologically in begetting children, but we only become
fully parents when we teach our children about God (1 Cor
4:15).

Gabriel's own name means "might of God." The might
of God treats Zechariah and Mary quite differently (Luke 1:18-
23, 1:34-38). This difference is based on the different understandings they displayed: Zechariah *doesn't believe* God can give
life through the marital act he performs with his wife. His reply
does not question his own ability to accomplish the creation of a
child, it questions God's ability – how could God make he and
Elizabeth fertile? Mary believes God can bring forth children
from her womb, she simply *doesn't understand* how she could become pregnant since she has never had sex (verse 34). Zechariah
essentially tells the angel he is doing his part, but questions God's
ability to do His part. Mary, on the other hand, is sure God can
accomplish whatever He wants, but she knows she is not doing
her part of the work. Is God calling her to do something she

had not intended to do? Zechariah's disbelief is silenced, Mary's belief is confirmed and enlightened.

The angel tells Zecheriah that John will live out a permanent vow as a Nazirite, as both Samson and Samuel did in the Old Testament. Nazirite vows did not have to be permanent, but anyone who was bound by such a vow was consecrated to the Lord for the length of the vow. We know that John kept it because Jesus alludes to that fact later in this Gospel (Lk 7:33).

The description of the Nazirite vow is contained in Num 6:1-21. The Nazirite vow is a rich foreshadowing of Jesus work on the Cross.

The Nazirite must (1) avoid wine and even grapes, (2) allow his hair to grow freely, (3) avoid dead bodies. Wine is a sign of joy, it prefigures Eucharist (Gen 27:25, Eccl 10:19, Sir 31:27-28). Jesus avoids drinking the fruit of the vine after celebrating the Last Supper, for He will be taking on the sorrow of mankind's sinfulness. He will drink it only on the point of death (John 19:30). The hair of the Nazirite reminds us of the hair of Esau (Gen 25:25-27). Esau's excessive hairiness was a sign of his animal tendencies, his sinful tendencies, his tendency to permit his appetites to control him and his destiny: a hungry Esau exchanged his birthright for a bowl of soup (Gen 25:29-34). The Nazirite growth of hair prefigures Christ taking on our sins on the Cross. Finally, death is the consequence of sin which Jesus alone takes upon Himself and conquers on the Cross. The Nazirite avoids the fruit of the vine, and grows in hairiness. Jesus avoids the fruit of the vine until the Father's Kingdom is established because He takes on our sins (Mt 26:29). The Nazirite avoids death because Christ will take on death for him.

The Nazirite purification after contact with a dead body foreshadows the Resurrection. If a Nazirite accidentally comes in contact with a dead body, he offers two pigeons and shaves his head on the seventh day, then offers a lamb on the eighth day. Pigeons, or doves, are signs of the Holy Spirit. Through the power of the Holy Spirit, Jesus descends into hell on the seventh day, and rises on the eighth day. He is the Lamb of God.

Upon the completion of the vow, the Nazirite offers a lamb for holocaust, a ewe for sin, a ram, and a cereal offering covered with oil. Jesus is the lamb of God who made a holocaust offering of Himself on the Cross, he did it for His Ewe, His Bride, the Church. The Nazirite ram recalls the ram offered when Abraham sacrificed his son Isaac. Since oil is a sign of the Holy Spirit, the cereal offering covered with oil is another foreshadowing of the Eucharist. After the vow is complete, the Nazirite shaves off his hair, signifying the removal of sin, and offers the shorn hair as a peace offering. He is given unleavened bread, and may again drink wine. After having our sins removed, we may again partake of Eucharist. Thus, in the completion of the vow, the Nazirite prefigures the establishment of the Eucharist.

Questions for study:
1. Why is naming important? Why should Christian parents choose to name our children after saints?
2. Why did the angel treated Zechariah and Mary differently?
3. Why is John's Nazirite vow important to his proclamation of Jesus?
4. How many different ways have the Incarnation and the Cross been foreshadowed in these first sixteen verses of Luke's Gospel?
5. From God's point of view, how is the Incarnation like the Crucifixion?

John the Baptist is Announced
1st week of Advent covers Luke 1:1-25
Session 5 – READ Luke 1:14-16

Catechism reference to Luke 1:15-19
717: A man sent by God

Scripture References and Themes
1:15 – **Nazirite vow** - Num 6:3, Lk 7:33, Jgs 13:4, 1 Sam 1:11 (LXX)

Like 80% of all the Old Testament references Jesus, His apostles, and His Scripture writers make in the New Testament, the angel's implicit Old Testament reference to 1 Samuel comes not from the Hebrew version of Scripture, but from the Greek version. The Hebrew version does not tell us that Samuel will avoid wine and liquor during his life, but the Greek version of Scripture does. The Greek version is sometimes called the Septuagint, which means "the seventy." It is often abbreviated LXX, i.e., the number "70" in Roman numerals. The name comes from the legend that the Hebrew Scriptures were translated into Greek by seventy Greek and Hebrew scholars around the year 250 BC. The differences between the Septuagint and the Hebrew Scriptures are important.

After the Babylonian Exile, 500 years prior to the birth of Christ, many of the Jews taken out of Israel decided not to return. Though they desired to maintain their faith, their descendants, like modern immigrants, learned the language of the country they lived in and forgot their native tongue, Hebrew. Due to Alexander the Great's conquests 300 years before the birth of Christ, everyone came to speak *koine*, or common, Greek – it was the language of trade. These Jews of the Babylonian Dispersion, who lived far from the Temple, wanted some way of maintaining their worship, and for them, the Hebrew Scriptures were translated into Greek. Subsequent writers of Scripture added to the Greek version without necessarily translating these newer Greek books back into Hebrew. As a result the Greek version of Jewish Scriptures has more books than the Hebrew version.

Likewise, the Greek version of the Scriptures, in books like Isaiah and 1 Samuel, have passages which differ, sometimes very much so, from the Hebrew version.

When the apostles went out into the world to explain the Scriptures to the Jews, and eventually to the Gentiles, they could not use the Hebrew Scriptures because neither audience understand Hebrew. Thus, the apostles always used the Greek. Even Jesus did this, for He quotes from the Septuagint far more often than He does from the Hebrew version of Scripture. The Catholic Bible is based on the Septuagint. Most other Christian Bibles are based on the Hebrew Scriptures. Thus, the Catholic Bible contains seven books Protestant Bibles do not (Tobit, Judith, Baruch, Wisdom, Sirach, 1 and 2 Maccabees) and longer versions of two other books (Daniel has a much longer chapter three, and three more chapters at the end, while Esther has six chapters unknown to the Protestant Bible).

Jewish leaders who had to deal with the growing Christian faith after the Resurrection ultimately decided to reject the Septuagint. They did not like having Scripture used to demonstrate the truth of Christ, and the books of the Septuagint were often quoted against them. They responded by saying those books were not inspired. Thus, the Catholic Bible is based on the Bible translation Jesus and the apostles preferred, while the Protestant Bible is based on the Scripture preferred by non-Christian Jews. While Jesus and the apostles did not quote from every book of either the Hebrew or the Greek Old Testament, and they clearly did not directly quote from any of the Septuagint books listed above, there are several implicit references to these Septuagint books in the New Testament, both in the Gospels and the epistles. If you are interested in learning more, read the section on Scripture in my book *Bible Basics*, Basilica Press, 2000.

Questions for study:
1.   Ancient Christians said, "The New Testament is hidden in the Old, while the Old Testament is revealed in the New." Think about all the foreshadowing we have seen so far, and explain, in your own words, what this phrase means.

2.   How does this understanding of how the two Testaments relate to one another help us understand the phrase, "The whole of Scripture talks about Christ"?

3.   When it comes to determining what books of Scripture are really part of Scripture, we have two choices. We can rely on the judgement of post-Christian Jews who do not recognize Christ as God, or on the judgement of early Christians led by the apostles and their successors, who were commissioned by Christ Himself. Which is more likely to be reliable? Why?

4.   According to the *Catechism*, how are Mary, Jesus, Elizabeth and John linked?

John the Baptist is Announced
1st week of Advent covers Luke 1:1-25
Session 6 – READ Luke 1:17-25

Catechism references to Luke 1:15-23
523: St. John the Baptist
718: The new Elijah
696: Fire, symbol of the Spirit
724: Mary manifests the Holy Spirit
716: The People of the poor
1070: What is liturgy?
717: A man sent by God
2684: The communion of saints

Scripture References and Themes
1:17 - **Spirit of Elijah** - Mal 3:1, 4:5, Sir 48:10, Mt 11:14, 17:13, Lk 3:23-24,
1:18 – Humility - Lk 1:34
1:19 – Gabriel - Dan 8:16, 9:21, Mt 18:10
1:20 – Belief - Lk 1:45
1:25 - **Removing reproach** - Gen 30:23, Is 4:1

Both Malachi and Sirach prophesied of the coming of John the Baptist, and Jesus confirmed that John did, indeed, carry the spirit of Elijah. Although John is perfectly correct to say that he is not Elijah, he carries the power Elijah did (John 1:21). Thus, the angel's words tell of the fulfillment of prophecy.

However, when we look at his words in verse 17, Gabriel also tells us something else. He speaks of John's ability to turn the hearts of fathers to the children and the disobedient to the just. Despite Gabriel's clear warning, Zechariah immediately fulfills the prophecy, because his own attitude towards God is one of disbelief and disobedience, that of a man who needs to be turned toward God by his own as-yet unconceived son. As a result, the angel silences him until he returns to obedience. While John's conception and birth ultimately converts Zechariah, his initial disbelief is in marked contrast to Mary's constant trust in the Lord.

Gabriel appears twice in the Old Testament, both times in Daniel. In every appearance, he explains to the recipient of the message what is to happen and how it is to be accomplished. In Matthew's Gospel, Jesus speaks of the angels who always see the face of God. Given Gabriel's words, we may assume he has some part among the angels Jesus described.

Gabriel's initial silence when he appeared to Zechariah near the altar, Zechariah's imposed silence and Elizabeth's decision to hide in silence all show how John's conception foreshadows the Incarnation. God takes flesh silently within the womb of Mary. Interestingly, the public reproach that pregnancy takes away from the barren Elizabeth will be added to the virgin Mary. In the Old Testament, Joseph was the first of only two sons Rachel bore; he was the son who removed her disgrace. He was also the son whom Israel loved above all his other sons, for Joseph was born of the woman he loved most. Likewise, John wipes away Elizabeth's disgrace and highlights the birth of the most beloved son of Israel, Jesus. Even in the wiping away of reproach, his birth has a dual meaning, for not only is Elizabeth's disgrace before men wiped away by the birth of John, but his ministry of preaching repentance will be the beginning of the wiping away of the disgrace of whole peoples.

Questions for study:
1. What is the connection between Elijah and John the Baptist?
2. Read Luke 9:7-8. What do the people think?
3. Consider Luke 9:19 and Matthew 17:3-13. What is the connection between Elijah, John, and Jesus?
4. How does the Catechism use these verses to explain the importance of John?
5. What does this passage tell us about Mary and the Holy Spirit?
6. What is "the communion of saints", and how does this passage demonstrate it?
7. Why is Elizabeth's comment about her son, John the Baptist, both a true statement and a prophecy?

Jesus is Announced to Mary

The Solemnity of the Annunciation is celebrated March 25th
2nd Week of Advent covers Luke 1:26-56
Session 1 - READ Luke 1:26-28

Catechism **references to Luke 1:26-28**
332: Angelic work
488: Mary's predestination
490-491: Immaculate Conception

Scripture References and Themes
1:27 – Jesus genealogy and virgin birth - Mt 1:16-18
1:28 – Prefigurements of Mary and Jesus - Jgs 6:12, Ruth 2:4, Jdt 13:18

Both Matthew and Luke agree that Mary was a virgin at the time of the child's conception, and that the conception took place through the power of the Holy Spirit. Given the apostolic emphasis on eyewitness accounts and personal testimony to the truth, this common emphasis on the facts surrounding Jesus' conception and birth serve as a powerful testimony to the accuracy of the record.

Luke could have opened this section of his narrative in any number of ways, but he chooses to do so through Elizabeth. The timing of the angel's appearance to Mary is not tied to events in the pagan world, but to events in the life of a daughter of Israel. The angel appears to Mary while Elizabeth is in her sixth month. Luke intends for us to see that Elizabeth and Mary are linked: what happens to the first is a living commentary on the life of the second. When we realize this, Luke 1:24, the verse from the previous week suddenly stands out in bright contrast. Elizabeth shows her humility for the great miracle done within her by hiding herself. In her own humility, she prefigures the immense humility of Mary, the handmaid of the Lord.

However, Elizabeth is not the only person in Scripture linked to Mary. The angel who greets Gideon uses words similar to those used to greet Mary. Upon closer examination, we discover that Gideon is the poorest family in his tribe, and the least among his family, both signals of humility. The offering Gideon makes, meat and bread, is the offering of the Cross – the flesh of God, who is the bread that comes down from heaven (John 6:48-51). Similarly, Boaz greets his reapers with another variation of the angel's greetings to Mary, recalling the words of Christ in John 4:35, 'the fields are white for harvest." Ruth left her parents and the land of her birth but comes under the protection of Boaz; Mary will come under the protection of Joseph and ultimately leave the land of Israel for Egypt. In yet another Old Testament correspondence, Judith, the most highly blessed woman in the Old Testament, cuts off the head of Israel's enemy through her pious reliance on the power of God. Mary, is the most highly blessed woman in the New Testament. Through her pious reliance on the power of God, she helps crush the head of the serpent. After all, she is the means through which God takes flesh and destroys Satan's power (Gen 3:15).

Questions for study:
1. Read Daniel 8:15-26, Daniel 9:20-27. Compare and contrast Gabriel's appearance in Daniel with Gabriel's appearance to Mary. What differences are there in the way Gabriel relates to one versus the other?
2. Many Christians reject the book of Judith. How does an increased understanding of Mary's role help us appreciate both Judith and the overall way God directed history so as to prefigure what He intended?
3. How has the *Catechism's* discussion of Mary enhanced your understanding of her role?

Jesus is Announced to Mary

The Solemnity of the Annunciation is celebrated March 25th
2nd Week of Advent covers Luke 1:26-56
Session 2 – READ Luke 1:28-30

Catechism references to Luke 1:28-30
490-491: Immaculate Conception
494-495: Obedience of Faith

Scripture References and Themes
1:30 – Greetings   - Lk 1:13

Gabriel does not just treat Daniel and Mary differently, he also treats Elizabeth, Zechariah, Joseph and Mary differently. No angel appears to Elizabeth at all. Joseph receives his angel in a dream (Mt 1:20). Zechariah's angel comes in answer to a prayer, while Mary's angel comes bearing a call to obedience. As he appears before Zechariah, Gabriel stands silent, but he addresses Mary immediately. His first words to Mary are words extolling her virtue, while his first words to Zechariah are simply words of reassurance. Thus, the angel's opening address to Mary can be seen not only as a mark of respect, but as a reminder to Mary of the great gifts God has given her as He asks her to obey Him. What God extols, man must also extol. Thus, Luke 1:28, taken together with Luke 1:42, compose the first half of the Hail Mary.

Mary is marked off as a particularly special woman, especially when we consider the matter of lineage. Luke takes pains to show us that Elizabeth and Zechariah are both descendants of noble lineage, while Mary's lineage is not clearly given. Yet despite this lack of evidence for noble lineage, Mary alone is greeted by the angel with the words: "Hail, full of grace!" The word used for "Hail!" – chairoo - is a royal greeting. This word is used only six times in Scripture: Matthew 26:48-49, where Judas betrays Jesus, Mark 15:18, John 19:3, and Matthew 27:29, where Roman soldiers mock Jesus' kingship, and Matthew 28:8-9, when the risen Jesus addresses the women outside the tomb. Judas uses the term in order to help convince the Roman soldiers that Jesus wants to be a temporal king, and the soldiers mock him with the term for the same reason. Jesus uses it to address the women after the Resurrection, because through His Resurrection they have become a royal priesthood, a holy nation, a people set apart (1 Peter 2:9). But here Gabriel uses the word to address someone who we do not know to be even of noble human lineage, much less worthy of royal treatment by an angel. The only royalty an angel recognizes is God. Why would he address a human person as royalty? Because in Israel, it is not the wife of the king who is the queen, rather, it is the mother of the king (2 Sam 12:24, 1 Kings 2:19). The angel addresses Mary as the Queen Mother of God, who will be her Son.

The angel follows the word "chairoo" with the title "kecharitomene", which means "full of grace" – the only person addressed in this manner in all of Scripture. Through this acclamation, we are brought to realize that Mary has been immaculately conceived, conceived in the fullness of grace, without any of that lack of grace that is sin. She is the first normal human being brought into existence since Adam and Eve were formed by the hand of God, the first since them to have the full measure of grace which every human is supposed to have, but which none of us do, because of the Fall. Mary, a daughter of Abraham and David, fulfills the prophecies made to both of them (Genesis 12:3 and 2 Samuel 7:12-16).

Questions for study:

1. Do the passages studied so far support the Catholic understanding of the Holy Family? How?
2. Have you ever prayed the Hail Mary as a conscious meditation on Scripture? Did it change your prayer life?
3. How has this session improved your understanding of the Immaculate Conception?
4. Compare the promises of mercy to Adam (Gen 3:15), Abraham (Gen 22:18), and David (2 Sam 7:12) with Luke 1:50. How has the promise grown and reached fulfillment in Jesus?

Jesus is Announced to Mary

The Solemnity of the Annunciation is celebrated March 25th
2nd Week of Advent covers Luke 1:26-56
Session 3 – READ Luke 1:30-33

Catechism **references to Luke 1:30-33**
430: Jesus – "God saves"
559: Jesus' Messianic entrance
709: Kingdom and Exile
2571: Abraham and faith
2812: God revealed in Jesus

Scripture References and Themes
1:31 - **Naming and child prophecy** - Lk 2:21, Mt 1:21, Gen 16:11, Jgs 13:3, Is 7:14
1:32 – **Kingship prophecy** - 2 Sm 7:12-13, 16, Is 9:7
1:33 – **Nations/authority** - Dan 2:44, 7:14; Mi 4:7, Mt 28:18

Mary and Joseph's obedience to God was complete – they would give to their son the name God had commanded. While Sara was commanded directly by God as to how to name her son (Gen 17:19), Hagar, Abram's concubine, was commanded by an angel as Mary was. God made covenant directly with Sara because she would bear the son of the Hebrew covenant, while He established His relationship with Ishmael, and therefore the rest of the world, through a messenger. God will call Isaac Abraham's "only son" (Gen 22:2). The Chosen People will come from the loins of Isaac, the child borne to Abraham by his wife Sarah.

Mary joins together the work of both Sarah and Hagar, for though approached by a messenger of God like Hagar, she would bear the son of the covenant within her womb, God takes flesh within her and she is His mother. The conception in Mary's womb is accomplished through the power of the Holy Spirit, thus fulfilling the prophecy of Isaiah 7:14. The promise made to David, the promise whose fulfillment was begun in Solomon, is completed in Jesus. He is the source upon which the everlasting throne of Israel stands. Isaiah's prophecy is coming to fulfillment.

Manoah's wife, the mother of Samson, was likewise visited by an angel. The angel tells her that Samson should be placed under a life-long Nazirite vow to consecrate him to the Lord. Samson's life prefigures that of Christ in several ways, but most importantly in the victory he gained over his opponents through his own death (Judges 16:28-30).

In Daniel, the prophecy of the kingdom of God is given to a pagan king in a prophetic dream. Though Daniel was only a prophet to the Chosen People, not the pagans, Daniel correctly interpreted the king's dream. The fact that this dream came through a pagan demonstrates that Jesus' work is the salvation of all mankind. Daniel himself will have a vision in which he sees Jesus being given dominion, and Micah confirmed the absolute authority Jesus' kingdom would have. Thus, when Christ tells us that he has been given all authority on heaven and on earth, we see that everything Gabriel told Mary is coming to pass.

Questions for study:
1. Ishmael was Abraham's circumcised son, yet God insisted only Isaac was the son of the covenant. What does this tell us about God's view of marriage?
2. Naming a person is a sign of parental authority over that person. How does this understanding affect our perception of Simon/Peter, the only person whom the God-man would rename?
3. The pagan king in Daniel dreamt Scripture. Why did God inspire pagans to participate in the composition of Scripture?
4. How have the *Catechism* references enhanced your understanding of Jesus?

Jesus is Announced to Mary

The Solemnity of the Annunciation is celebrated March 25th
2nd Week of Advent covers Luke 1:26-56
Session 4 – READ Luke 1:34-45

Catechism references to Luke 1:34-45

64: Work of prophets	148: Mary, obedience, faith
269: The Holy Spirit	273: God's power
276: Almighty God	437: The Shepherds
448: The Title "Lord"	484: The Annunciation
486: The Christ	494-495: Obedience of Faith
497: Virginal conception	505: Men as sons of God
510: Perpetual virginity	523: St. John the Baptist
697: Cloud/light	717: John, precursor
2617: Prayer of Mary	2675-2677: Mary cooperates
2827: Worshippers	2856: Amen

Scripture References and Themes
1:34 – Hubris vs. humility - Lk 1:18
1:35 – Messengers - Mt 1:20
1:37 – God's power - Gen 18:14, Jer 32:37, Mt 19:26
1:41 – Fulfillment - Lk 1:15
1:42 – Blessedness - Lk 11:27-28, Jgs 5:24, Jdt 13:18, Dt 28:4
1:45 – Humility rewarded - Lk 1:20

As was discussed in Luke 1:18 last week, Zechariah's answer to the angel displays a real impudence and lack of faith which cannot be found in Mary's reply. The angel's treatment of Joseph is in marked contrast to Zechariah. The angel tells both Mary and Joseph the same thing – what is happening to Mary is through the indwelling of God. Joseph, being a devout Jew, would instantly recognize that if his vision is accurate, Mary has met God more intimately than anyone in history. The Holy of Holies in the Temple was a place so sacred that only the high priest could enter it, and only once a year. Before he entered, a rope was tied around his ankle, so if he suddenly died while he was within he could be dragged out, for no one else could enter the sacred place. Mary was made sacred by God, and Joseph recognizes what this means.

The sacredness of God is constantly emphasized through-out Scripture. Moses spoke to God as a man speaks to a man, and had to veil his face after these conversations, because it shone so brightly that no man could look upon him (Ex 33:11,34:33-35). If Mary carried God's Son through the power of God, than God had graced her more intimately than anyone in history. Joseph would no more attempt to have sexual relations with someone touched to such depths by Divinity than he would attempt to enter the Holy of Holies.

During the course of his life, Abram was shown that with God, nothing is impossible. The whole people of Israel was shown the same thing: God gathered them from where they had been scattered, and again formed them into a nation. Jesus will echo the words of the angel during his own ministry, when He explains that salvation is truly open to all. This salvation is made open only through Jesus, who came to us through Mary.

Mary mediates Jesus to John and Elizabeth. Just as Moses was a mediator of God's word to the world, Mary also medi-ates God's Word to the world, for it is only when she brings Christ to Elizabeth and to John, still in the womb, that both are filled with the Holy Spirit and Luke 1:15 is fulfilled. God is the source of grace, and Jesus is the sole mediator between God and man. However, through the power of God, "we are God's co-workers" (1 Cor 3:9). Each one of us, through our being joined to the Body of Christ, assists Jesus in His work of media-tion between God and man. Mary, being the Queen Mother of God, does the co-working proper to human persons to a uniquely excellent degree.

Mary agreed to do the will of God. Like the angel, Elizabeth knows that Mary, unlike her husband, Zechariah, has always believed the word of the Lord. Elizabeth fulfills the words of Deuteronomy and of Christ by blessing her here. Mary is more blessed than Jael, who drove a tent peg through the head of an enemy of Israel, more blessed than Judith, who cuts off the head of an enemy of Israel. By hearkening to the voice of the Lord, Mary fulfills the promise God had made to Israel in the time of Moses, that the fruit of a woman's womb would be blessed.

Incidentally, the Angelus, a prayer of the Church prayed three times a day, at 6 a.m., noon and 6 p.m., is based on Luke 1:26-39.

Questions for study:

1. Compare the overshadowing in Exodus 40:34-36, Exodus 24:15-16, Luke 1:35, and Luke 9:34-35. Why is it appropriate for the ark, Mary and Jesus each to be overshadowed?

2. The ark of the covenant held the rod of Aaron, which performed the first four miracles before Pharoah, the Ten Commandments, and a bag of manna (Heb 9:4). Mary carries the power of God, the Logos – the Word of God and the Bread from heaven. In your own words, explain why Mary is called, "the Ark of the New Covenant."

3. Mary, like every human person, is a co-worker with God. God's work is our salvation. What verse says "we are God's co-workers"? Why can we say that every human person is a co-redeemer with Christ?

4. Genesis 3:15 talks about crushing the serpent's head. Who prefigures this action in the Old Testament?

5. Have you ever attempted to add the Angelus to your prayer routine? How might it help if you did?

Jesus is Announced to Mary

The Solemnity of the Annunciation is celebrated March 25th
2nd Week of Advent covers Luke 1:26-56
Session 5 – READ Luke 1:46-49

Catechism references to Luke 1:46-49

148: Mary, obedience, faith   273: God's power
722-723: Mary, full of grace   971: All call her blessed
2097: Adoration   2599: Jesus prays
2619: The Magnificat   2675-2677: Mary cooperates
2807: His hallowed name   2827: God's worshippers

Scripture references and Themes
1:46 – Soul's rejoicing - Ps 35:9, Is 61:10
1:46-55 – Hannah's Song - 1 Sam 2:1-10
1:47 – God's glory - 1 Tim 2:3, Tit 2:10, 3:4, Jude 25
1:48 – Affliction and blessing - Lk 11:27, 1 Sm 1:11, 2 Sm
16:12, 2 Kings 14:26, Ps 113:7
1:49 – Great redeeming work - Dt 10:21, Pss 71:19, 111:9,
126:2-3

The echo of Psalm 35:9, especially given the context
which the Psalm provides, gives us a hint of what life must have
been like for Mary, especially during her unexpected pregnancy.
Yet her words also echo Isaiah, reminding us that she bears the
salvation which God promised all men.

Hannah's song of praise at the birth of Samuel is the foundation upon which Mary built her song, the Magnificat, although
Mary's song is robust in a way that Hannah's is not. Hannah's
song concentrates on her own victory ("I have swallowed up
my enemies") while Mary's song concentrates on the power of
the Lord ("He has shown the strength of His arm"). Hannah's
song concentrates on the here and now, while Mary sees the
broad sweep of salvation history, and God working through it
all. This is, in part, why every consecrated person must pray the
Magnificat every evening as part of the Liturgy of the Hours.

However, Hannah's story definitely echoes important events
in the life of Jesus and His Body, the Church. Both Hannah and

the apostles near Pentecost pray earnestly to God. Hannah is accused of being drunk by Eli (1 Sam 1:13-14), and the 120 are called drunkards by the crowd after the descent of the Spirit (Acts 2:13). She who was barren is, through the power of God, made fertile, just as the Church is made fertile through the descent of the same Holy Spirit who first overshadowed Mary here at the Annunciation. Just as Eli's sons, the priests who serve the Temple, lose their place to Samuel through abuse of power, so the Pharisees and scribes who "sit in the seat of Moses" (Mt 23:2-3) lose their place to Jesus and the apostles. Samuel and Jesus both increase before God, while the others decrease. What Hannah and Samuel prefigure, Jesus and His Church is.

God is Mary's saviour as much as He is ours, for without His grace, she would have been a sinner. The grace Christ won for every person on the Cross was as necessary for her sinlessness as they are for us if we are to successfully avoid sin. Thus, what the woman in the crowd uttered about Jesus' mother was prophecied by Mary herself.

Hannah had already prefigured part of the role Mary was to play. David similarly prefigures Christ. David's own son sought to kill David. God's created sons and daughters sought to kill Him and ultimately succeeded. The man cursing David in 2 Samuel prefigures the curses Christ will endure. Just as God saved Israel through Jeroboam, He will save Israel through Jesus, only in a far superior way. Mary, a lowly handmaid, is here lifted up from the dust and set over kings and princes. Her King is her son, the Lord of Lords, Jesus Christ.

The Deuteronomy passage speaks of the establishment of the priesthood of Levi, the magnificent works of the Lord, the need to care for the stranger, and the way God has brought increase to Israel. Through the Incarnation, a new priesthood will be established, God will do greater works than every before, salvation will be opened to every human person, and the Church, God's Chosen People, will increase throughout the ages. The Psalm 71 reference is interesting because the way the Faith has been practiced by the Chosen People is now in its twilight. Jesus will bring Judaic practice and belief to its fullness in a new and vibrant way. Psalm 111 is a beautiful praise of the magnificent work of the Lord, of which Mary is the most perfect human example. Likewise, Psalm 126 speaks of the great joy that belongs to the Mother of God.

Questions for study:

1. Compare Hannah's song and Mary's Magnificat. What similarities do you see? What differences do you see? How has your understanding of Mary's role been enhanced by the *Catechism* references above?

2. How is the hallowing of God's name radically different from the blessing of Mary's?

3. We have now seen that the infancy narrative contains three important prayers of the Church: the Hail Mary, the Angelus and the Magnificat. Why is this part of Scripture such a rich source of prayer for the Church?

Jesus is Announced to Mary

The Solemnity of the Annunciation is celebrated March 25th
2nd Week of Advent covers Luke 1:26-56
Session 6 – READ Luke 1:50-56

Catechism references to Luke 1:50-56
422: God sent His Son
706: Spirit of promise
2465: God, source of all truth.

Scripture references and Themes
1:50 – God's steadfast love - Psalms 89:2, 103:13-17
1:51 – Victory - Psalms 89:10, 118:15, Jer 32:17
1:52 – Rich vs. Poor - 1 Sam 2:7, 2 Sam 22:28, Job 5:11, Ps 147:6, Sir 10:14, James 4:6, 1 Pet 5:5
1:53 – Filled vs. Hungry - 1 Sam 2:5, Psalms 107:9
1:54 – Power of God - Psalm 98:3, Is 41:8-9
1:55 – The Covenants - Gen 13:15, 17:7, 18:18, 22:17-18, Mi 7:20

Psalm 89 reminds us of the covenant established with David and speaks of the marvelous attributes of God, the joy of those who follow Him. Psalm 103 is interesting because it contains a thumbnail description of Mary's Immaculate Conception (103:4). Most of us were saved from the pit of original sin by being pulled out of it by the grace won by Christ on the Cross. Mary, however, was saved from it by being pulled away from the edge of that pit before she ever fell into it. That is, she was given the unmerited grace of being free from original sin from the moment of her conception. This psalm also deals with the problem of pain (103:10). Our sins are the cause of the pain in the world. As John Cardinal Newman observed, the smallest venial sin rocks the foundations of the created world. Thus, when we see a disaster that causes untold suffering, we are seeing the result of a small venial sin. When we consider the vast sinfulness of the human race, it becomes clear that God shields us from the vast majority of the pain that would otherwise be present in the world. He permits us to taste a small amount just so we can gain some understanding of what it is we do to ourselves through sin. Thus, the question is not, "Why does God permit so much pain in the world," rather, it is, "Why isn't there *more* pain?" Given the suffering God will experience in the flesh, Mary's invocation of this psalm tells us an enormous amount about the Incarnation.

The strength of the Lord's arm, and the fact of His victory are attested to by the Psalms and by Jeremiah, while the songs of Hannah, David and Job as well as the proverbs of Sirach each repeat Mary's theme – God pays attention to the lowly. This theme continues in the New Testament, with the letters from James and Peter. God's attention to the poor and lowly is most greatly exemplified in Mary, who is nothing but a poor handmaid, a lowly daughter of Israel. Psalm 107 repeats the idea that praise to the Lord is the proper prayer of the redeemed. Mary's prayerful reflection on this psalm merely re-emphasizes how God redeemed her, guarding and guiding her by the straight path of grace to the heavenly city.

Psalm 98 will be alluded to by Christ Himself as He enters Jerusalem. When questioned on why He permits His followers to praise Him so highly, He replies that if they were silenced the very rocks would shout out the same words (Luke 19:40). Meanwhile, Isaiah's prophecy speaks of Israel as God's servant, and tells us that Israel's victory will be brought about by God Himself. In the Incarnation, we see this prophecy brought to fulfillment, for Mary, the handservant of the Lord and a daughter of Israel, is the conduit through which God's victory comes. The promise God made to Abraham so long ago is strongly attested to in the Old Testament. With the Annunciation and Incarnation, the promises have reached fulfillment. In the Church today, the truth of the promise and the prophecy are borne out, for the Christian Faith has spread to every nation and is spreading even now within every nation.

Questions for Study:
1. Does today's study enhance your understanding of how Mary was immaculately conceived yet still in need of God's saving power? How?
2. Does it enhance your understanding of why there is so much

pain in the world? Could you explain this concept to anyone who asked you about the problem of pain?

3.   Why can we say that Mary is, in a certain sense, the person who speaks for all Israel?

4.   The *Catechism* references Luke 1:26-56 far more often than any other passage we will study. Why is it such a rich resource for Christian doctrine?

Jesus is Announced to Joseph
3rd Week of Advent covers Matthew 1:1-25
Session 1 – READ Matthew 1:1-19

Catechism references to Matthew 1:1-19
437: The Shepherds
497: Virginal conception of Christ

Scripture references and Themes
1:1 – Genealogy - Gen 5:1, 22:18; 1 Chr 17:11
1:2 – Lk 3:23-28, Gen 21:3, 25:26, 29:35, 1 Chr 2:1
1:3-7 – Gn 38:29-30, Ru 4:18-20, 1 Chr 2:4-15, 3:5-15, 2 Sam 12:24
1:11-12 – 2 Kings 24:14, Jer 27:20, 1 Chro 3:16-19
1:18 – Mary's story - Lk 1:26-38

Luke reminds us that Jesus is the son of David and Abraham, but Genesis reminds us that everyone is a son of Adam. Indeed, all of Scripture can be seen as nothing more than an account of how the sons of Adam live out their relationship with God. The genealogy given in Luke differs in some respects from that given in Matthew. At least two explanations can be advanced as to why these differences occur. The first may be associated with the Levirite requirement that the brother of any married man who dies childless must have relations with his dead brother's widow until a child is produced, so that the dead man's name might live on in the history of the Chosen People. Thus, Matthew's listing may be of Jesus' "official" fathers, while Luke's listing is of the actual biological fathers. The second explanation for the difference may be that Luke is actually listing Mary's genealogy, not Joseph's. This possibility is hinted at in the introduction given by Luke "He was the son, as was thought, of Joseph…"

Matthew's geneology reminds us that four of the women - Tamar, (Genesis 38, 1 Chronicles 2:4), Rahab (Joshua 2:6,17), Bathsheba (2 Samuel 11:12,24) and Ruth – were foreigners, some with rather disreputable characters. In this way, Matthew reminds us that God intends to save all men, not just the Chosen People.

He also reminds us that what may seem disreputable – a woman pregnant yet unmarried, for instance – can still be part of God's plan.

Luke's description of the birth is much more involved than is Matthew's. While Luke concentrated on Mary's story, Matthew concentrates on Joseph's. Thus, Luke takes a dozen verses to tell us about Mary's encounter with Gabriel but says virtually nothing about Joseph, while Matthew summarizes Mary's story in a single verse, but spends over a dozen verses telling us about Joseph.

Though Scripture is quite good about telling us these details, it does not tell us something which is crucial to our understanding of Jesus, namely, how did the divine nature and human nature become joined? We must first understand the difference between nature and person. A person is a "who", a nature is a "what". If something rustles in the darkness and you ask, "What is that?" you are asking about its nature. If you ask "Who is that?", you are asking about the person. The nature defines the range of possible actions, the person is the one who performs the actions.

How does a person perform an action? Every person possesses an intellect and a will. The intellect knows, the will chooses. There are only three kinds of persons, that is, three kinds of intellect and will. There is the divine intellect and will, angelic intellect and will, and human intellect and will.

The divine nature is the one divine intellect with the one divine will. Since the definition of a person is "one who possesses an intellect and a will," it is necessarily the case that each Person of the Trinity totally possesses the one divine intellect and the one divine will to Himself. He does not share it with the other two. How can there be Three Persons each totally possessing the one divine intellect and one divine will? That isn't entirely clear. We just know that all three Persons know with the same mind and choose with the same will. For this reason, there is never any opposition or discord between the Persons of the Trinity.

Human nature is the human intellect, with its human will, united to a human body. The human intellect and will are together called the soul, so it is correct (although redundant) to say human nature is made up of the human intellect, will, soul and body. The intellect knows, the will chooses, the body is the medium through which the soul interacts with the world.

The Son of God took on the title "Jesus" (which means "God saves") by taking on a full human nature in His own Person. This means Jesus, the Son of God, not only has a body, but he also has two intellects and two wills, one each of the divine and the human. His human intellect and will is finite, like any man's, but His divine intellect and will are infinite. This is why Jesus could say, "The Father is greater than I" (Jn 14:28). God the Father is greater than the human nature the Son took on, even though Son and Father are equal in divinity. Jesus always knew He was God in His divine intellect, but His human intellect had to grow, mature, and become capable of handling more and more over time, because that is how humans are made. We grow. Because He is the Second Person of the Trinity, with complete control over nature, His human intellect and will is never in opposition to His divine intellect and will, rather they always work harmoniously together. His human intellect and will are simply infinitely weaker than His divine intellect and will.

Since death is simply the separation of the soul from the body, this understanding of the Incarnation also explains why the universe didn't disappear when God died. Just as our human soul continues to exist after the separation that is death, so Jesus' human soul separated from His human body, but both continued to exist. His divine intellect and divine will, which were always joined to both His body and His human soul, simply brought his human soul and human body back into union after three days in the tomb. The Incarnation, death and Resurrection were as simple as joining your own two hands, unjoining them, and then joining them back together – from God's point of view, at least.

Questions for study:
1. Which of the four foreigners in Matthew's genealogy were rather disreputable? What does this tell us?
2. How does Matthew's narrative of the infancy provide a perfect counterpart to Luke's narrative?
3. Has your understanding of the Incarnation been enhanced by this session? If so, how?

4. Given the correct understanding of the divine nature, why would it be wrong to say that the Father poured out His wrath on the Son as He hung on the Cross?

5. Catholics know that "Jesus is the Son of God. The Son of God exists from all eternity to all eternity, but Jesus came into existence at a specific point in time." Think of the different ways your parents can be addressed. Which names and roles have they always had, and which names and roles did they permanently take on at specific moments in time? How does this help you understand Jesus?

Jesus is Announced to Joseph
3rd Week of Advent covers Matthew 1:1-25
Session 2 – READ Matthew 1:20-25

Catechism references to Matthew 1:20-25
333: Angelic work   430: Jesus – "God saves"
437: The Shepherds   452: The name of Jesus
486: The Christ   497: Virginal conception
744: Preparing His way   1846: Mercy and Sin
1507: Heal the sick   2666: Prayer in Jesus' name
2812: God revealed in Jesus

Scripture references and Themes
1:20 – Dreams and the Spirit - Mt 2:13-19, Lk 1:35
1:21 – Jesus and salvation - Lk 2:21, Jn 1:29, Acts 5:31, 13:23
1:23 – Virgin birth - Is 7:14 (LXX)
1:25 – Childbirth - Lk 2:7

Joseph information about the origin of the pregnancy is the same as Mary's, but he receives the information in a more indirect way, through a dream. Zechariah, father of John the Baptist, was directly informed of his wife's coming pregnancy by an angel, but Joseph is instructed exclusively through dreams (Mt 1:20, 2:12, 2:13, 2:19, and 2:22). This recalls the Joseph of the Old Testament, who both dreamed prophetic dreams and correctly interpreted the meanings of dreams. In a certain sense, Joel's prophecy (2:28 or 3:1) quoted by Peter in Acts 2:17, is already being fulfilled here in Matthew: "your young men shall see visions and your old men shall dream dreams."

While John's name was made known only to Zechariah, both Mary and Joseph were told what name is to be given to the son she bore. Matthew tells us that Joseph is the one who bore the responsibility for naming the child. What is foretold by the angel is confirmed the first time John the Baptist sees Jesus, and re-confirmed by Paul and Peter, in separate speeches in Acts. Each name Jesus the savior of Israel.

Interestingly, the Hebrew version of the fulfilled prophecy of Isaiah 7:14 says that a woman (almah) will be with child, while the Greek version says a virgin (parthenos) will be with child. By recalling the Greek version of Isaiah 7:14 and remembering Isaiah's prophecy of a painless birth (Isaiah 66:6), we find a small part of the beginning of the doctrine of Mary's perpetual virginity: virgin before, during and after the birth of Jesus.

The angel's words reminds us that Joseph is of David's line (1:20). When Joseph "called his name Jesus" (Matt 1:25), he was by that act declaring his true fatherhood of Jesus, not in the biological sense, but in the sense that Joseph will care for Jesus, helping Jesus conform His human will and intellect to His Divine will and intellect. Thomas Aquinas and Pope John Paul II point out that our biological parenthood begins the work of parenthood, but does not complete it. Parenthood is perfected only when we bring our children to full understanding of God. Though Jesus possessed the Divine intellect, and therefore always knows He is God, still there was a way in which Joseph truly helped Him grow in His human knowledge so that it was capable of always fully understanding His own divinity. Jesus, the only son of Joseph and Mary, could therefore truly call him "father."

Some mistakenly think the word "until" in Matthew 1:25 shows Joseph had marital relations with Mary after Jesus' birth, even to the point of Mary conceiving and bearing more children. Matthew, however, intended no such meaning, and the Hebrew understanding of "until" does not support such a meaning. In Genesis 8:5, the waters receded "until the mountain tops were seen." and in 1 Corinthians 15:25 Jesus reigns "until all enemies are under his feet." In both of those passages, "until" simply describes an important event in an on-going process. The process continues regardless of the event. Similarly, the "until" here does not indicate that Joseph had relations with Mary after the birth of Jesus, nor does any other passage of Scripture lend credence to the idea. Even the phrase "brothers of Christ", common to the New Testament, is used to mean "cousins," not biological brothers. Hebrew, which is a tribal language, has no word for brother. Any two people descended from the same patriarch (e.g., Levi, Benjamin, Judah, etc.) were considered to be "brothers."

Furthermore, in the Hebrew tradition, a woman found to

be with child that is not her husband's is forbidden forevermore both to him and to the man who impregnated her. Intercourse was permitted during the betrothal period, but Matthew clearly indicates Joseph did not engage in it. If he had done so during the betrothal, he would have been declaring Jesus to be his biological son. By not doing so, Joseph was shown to be a pious Jew who lived by the Law. Since he refrained from intercourse before Jesus' birth, he would necessarily have done so afterwards as well.

Questions for study:
1. Why is the naming of Jesus an important event, especially in light of Joseph's fatherhood of Jesus?
2. Using the information provided in the sessions studied so far, explain in your own words why Joseph could not have violated Mary's virginity.
3. Why does God communicate with Joseph only through dreams?
4. How has the *Catechism* enhanced your knowledge of the Incarnation?

John the Baptist is Born

Feast of John the Baptist's birth is celebrated June 24th

3rd Week of Advent covers Matthew 1:1-25

Session 3 – READ Luke 1:57-60

Scripture references and Themes

1:58 – Joy of birth - Lk 1:14

1:59 – Circumcision - Gen 17:10-12, Lev 12:3-4, Lk 2:21

Luke's painstaking attention to detail shines forth in this passage, as he records the fulfillment of the angel's prophecy concerning the joy exhibited at John's birth. The joy of birth and children are a constant theme throughout Scripture, for we image God's own fruitfulness through the sexual act in marriage. God is a family of persons, the family after whom every family is named (Eph 3:15). Covenants create families. The first covenants between God and Adam and between God and Noah were both marked by the command towards fruitful sexual union (Gen 1:28, 9:1, 7). Jacob was likewise commanded by both his father, Isaac, and God Himself to be fruitful and multiply (Gen 28:3, 35:11) and part of the proof of God's covenant with Israel is precisely her fruitfulness (Lev 26:9, Jer 23:3). Insofar as anyone actively attempts to destroy the fruitfulness of marriage, they actively attempt to destroy the very image of God inscribed by God into their own bodies.

Given God's emphasis on fecundity, the sign of circumcision for the covenant is quite interesting. Genesis describes circumcision as the outward mark of the covenant between God and Abram. The sign of circumcision prefigured the power of baptism (Col 2:11-12), which is salvation (1 Peter 3:21). The Leviticus passage goes on to explain why the Church's feast of the Presentation of the Lord is so far removed from the Feast of the Circumcision. Once the feast of the birth of God is set, the feast of circumcision must follow Christmas eight days later, and the presentation must follow thirty-three days after that. In times past, it was a custom for Christian women who had given birth to go through a "churching" ceremony reminiscent of the purification of Mary and Jesus. This liturgical rite was the Church's way of reminding all families that we are made in the image of the Holy Family, and that the Holy Family is made in the image of God (Eph 3:14-15).

Genesis 17:10-14 and Leviticus 12:3 provide us with the Hebrew rules on circumcision. Once the male child was circumcised, that child was responsible for keeping the whole law of Moses, all the food regulations, the clothing regulations, the regulations on washing, sacrifices, offerings – everything. Acts 15:1-29 shows Peter describing what a burden circumcision and the law of Moses placed on the Hebrews. Paul tells the Galatians this as well, in Galatians 5:2-6 and Galatians 6:12-16. But in Colossians 2:11-13, Paul makes an interesting connection. He says that circumcision and baptism are linked, and in Romans 6:4, Paul explicitly links baptism with the crucifixion. Putting all these references together, we see that God gave circumcision to the Hebrews in order to show them how impossible it is for man to save himself. At the same time, "circumcision on the eighth day" foreshadows the work of Christ on the Cross. Because the Sabbath day was called the seventh day, for on this day God rested, and because Jesus' Sunday resurrection gave power to baptism, Christians have long associated the number "eight" with the sacrament of baptism and with salvation itself. God shows that what is impossible for men is possible for God. The Old Testament ritual surrounding circumcision is God's hint to us of what the Cross would both mean and accomplish.

Questions for Study:

1. Eight persons were saved in Noah's ark. A baptistery is an eight-sided buildings where baptisms are performed. Why eight persons for Noah and eight sides for the baptistry?

2. Church architecture and art have long been used as a teaching tool. How much do you know about the architecture of your own church? How might a study of architecture and art complement Scripture study?

3. How does contraception, either permanent surgical sterilization or temporary chemical or physical barriers, violate the image of the I AM which we carry in our bodies and in our family?

4. If Christmas is Dec 25, when are the Feasts of the Annunciation and birth of John the Baptist?

John the Baptist is Born

Feast of John the Baptist's birth is celebrated June 24th

3rd Week of Advent covers Matthew 1:1-25

Session 4 – READ Luke 1:60-67

Scripture references and Themes

1:63 – Naming John - Lk 1:13

1:64 – Imposed silence - Lk 1:20

Zechariah, who has learned obedience to God through the silence imposed upon him, names his son as the angel of the Lord had commanded. Notice that Zechariah plays a part in his own return to speech. If he had not worked with the grace God sent through the angel, that is, if he had not been obedient, he would have remained speechless. As it was, he embraced the grace of the moment and was restored. Grace does not replace nature, rather, it builds on nature. God provides us the power to accomplish a thing, and we – by our obedience and embrace of that grace – are lifted to a much higher plane than we would otherwise have access to. Even our decision to embrace grace is itself a grace from God, a gift of inestimable value. Zechariah was graced by the angel's presence and he was graced to be able to act as the angel commanded. This is the mysterious interplay between free will and God's power. Everything we accomplish is accomplished only through the grace of God, yet we really do have a choice in whether to participate in that grace. Our will is always entirely free.

In a certain sense, Zechariah's unwillingness to believe the angel is linked to the Apostle Thomas' unwillingness to believe that Jesus is truly risen from the dead (John 20:24-29). Zechariah is engaging in the marital act with his wife, but doesn't believe that God actually has the power to make the act bring forth new life. Thomas watched Jesus raise Lazarus from the dead - in fact, it is Thomas who exhorts the apostles to accompany Jesus to Lazarus' tomb (John 11:16) – yet he is unable to believe that Jesus can raise himself to new life (John 20:24-29). Thus, Zechariah's story is linked to what Luke tells us about both the Resurrection and Pentecost. When the angel first came to

Zechariah, fear fell upon him (Luke 1:12). After Zechariah re-
gains the ability to speak, fear fell upon all of his neighbors (Luke
1:65). When the apostles first see the risen Christ, fear falls upon
them (Luke 24:37), when they speak at Pentecost, those who
listen are cut to the heart (Acts 2:37). In Zechariah's confirmation
that his son's name will be John, which means "God is gracious", God is telling us that we will see more of his grace being
poured out, if only we pay attention to events.

While we completed our study of the Magnificat's content last week, no study of the Magnificat during Advent would
be complete without mention of the 'O! antiphons." The "O
Antiphons" are a seven different antiphons used in the Liturgy
of the Hours. Each is prayed in turn on seven consecutive nights
before and after the Magnificat, starting Dec 17. They are meant
to bring us to deeper contemplation of God's love for us. These
are the antiphons, along with their Scriptural basis, if you would
like to incorporate them into your own prayer:

O WISDOM, who came from the mouth of the Most
High, reaching from end to end and ordering all things mightily
and sweetly: Come, and teach us the way of prudence. *Sirach
24:2; Wisdom 8:1.*

O LORD AND RULER of the House of Israel, who
appeared to Moses in the flame of the burning bush and gave
him the law on Sinai: Come, and redeem us with outstretched
arm. *Exodus 3:2, 20:1.*

O ROOT OF JESSE, who stands for a sign of the people,
before whom kings shall keep silence and unto whom the Gentiles shall make supplication: Come to deliver us, and tarry not.
Isaiah 11:1-3.

O KEY OF DAVID, and Sceptre of the House of Israel, who
opens and no man shuts, who shuts and no man opens: Come,
and bring forth the captive from his prison, he who sits in darkness and in the shadow of death. *Isaiah 22:22.*

O DAWN OF THE EAST, brightness of the light eternal, and Sun of Justice: Come, and enlighten them that sit in darkness and in the shadow of death. *Psalm 19:6-7.*

O KING OF THE GENTILES and their desired One, the Cornerstone that makes both one: Come, and deliver man, whom You formed out of the dust of the earth. *Psalm 2:7-8, Ephesians 2:14-20.*

O EMMANUEL, God with us, our King and Lawgiver, the expected of the nations and their Savior: Come to save us, O Lord our God. *Isaiah 7:14; 33:22.*

Questions for Study:
1.   Zechariah's attitude brought him hardship. When has God's kindness seemed harsh to you?
2.   Some Christians describe grace as a free gift, but don't fully appreciate its transforming power. How is Zechariah's situation an example of the power grace has to transform the inner man?
3.   The links between Zechariah and Thomas also point to links between child-bearing and Christ's death and resurrection. How is the deliberate destruction of one's own fertility a lived lack of faith in God?
4.   Imagine the interaction between Zechariah and Elizabeth, from the moment Zechariah sees the angel at the altar to the moment his tongue is loosed. How would you have dealt with such a situation

John the Baptist is Born
Feast of John the Baptist's birth is celebrated June 24th
3rd Week of Advent covers Matthew 1:1-25
Session 5 – READ Luke 1:68-75

Catechism references to Luke 1:68-73
422: God has visited His people
706: Spirit of promise
717: John, precursor, prophet, baptist

Scripture references and Themes
1:68 – Blessed be the Lord - Lk 7:16, Pss 41:13, 72:18, 106:48, 111:9
1:69, 71 – Horns - Joshua 6:20, 1 Sam 16:1, 1 Kings 1:50-51, Ps 18:3, 106:10
1:72 – Covenant - Gen 17:7, Lev 26:42, Ps 105:8-9, Mi 7:20
1:73 – Isaac offered - Gen 22:16-17
1:75 – Renounce the world - Ti 2:12

Zechariah's first words are the words his son will pro-claim about Jesus, and the words the multitude will proclaim as well, words that echo several of the Psalms. Zechariah's blessing of the Lord recall the Psalmist's description of the many hard-ships suffered by those who desire to do God's will, but who find their own hardness of heart interfering with their ability to do so. The silence he endured was like a little death, for death is the result of disobedience and we are silent in the grave (Psalm 94:17). Psalm 72 recalls the glory of Solomon, and Zechariah's son will proclaim the coming of someone greater than Solomon. Psalm 106 recalls the entire history of Israel, and his son will proclaim the one who has guided Israel through it all. This is why Psalm 111 describes the glory of the deeds of the Almighty. The Psalms referenced, when taken together, describe the hard-ship and the mission of John the Baptist.

Zechariah speaks of the horn of salvation, and it is use-ful to think about the many different ways horns were put into service in Israel. Horns were used to signal the armies; in this sense, John the Baptist is a living horn for Jesus. They were used as vessels for wine and oil, the first being a sign of the Eucharist and the second a sign of the Spirit. They were also attached to the altar that stood before the ark of the covenant. Any guilty man who seized the horns of the altar was safe from summary execution, just as anyone who seizes on John's message will be brought to the beginning of the work of salvation.

Zechariah reminds those listening that God has made covenant and will not forget it. Abraham offered Isaac, his only son, to God, in a prefigurement of the death of Jesus Christ. As a result, God established a permanent covenant with him and his descendants. Zechariah's son will be the last and greatest prophet, for he will announce the completion of the covenant: it is completed in the person of Jesus Christ.

Malachi 4:5 prophecies the coming of the one who is identified in Luke 1:76, and Luke 7:26 specifically makes the connection between Malachi's prophecy and this fulfillment. Similarly, Isaiah 9:2 and Luke 1:79 are very closely linked passages, Isaiah prophesying what Luke fulfills. Thus, Zechariah is telling his listeners the whole Old Testament has been pointing to the events that are happening in front of them. Like Mary's Magnificat, which is prayed by all religious every evening in the prayer called "The Liturgy of the Hours," Zechariah's canticle (verses 68-79), called the Benedictus, is likewise an integral part of the Liturgy of the Hours. It is prayed every morning by all consecrated Catholics and many lay Catholics besides. Together, morning prayer, with the Benedictus at its center, and evening prayer, with the Magnificat at its center, are called the "hinge prayers", the prayers upon which all other prayers of the Liturgy of the Hours depend.

Questions for study:

1. Name three ways in which "horn of salvation" is meant to help us understand the saving work of God.
2. If Abraham and his son prefigured the death of Christ and if John is the greatest prophet, what can we expect not only his words, but his whole life, to prefigure?
3. Since Jesus is the head and the Church is the Body, what kind of death would John likely experience, if he is living out the life of Christ? What kind of death did he actually

experience (Mt 14:10)? How do events like this affect your understanding of how to read Scripture?

4. Why would the Church choose to make the Benedictus and the Magnificat the heart of her daily prayer?

5. How do the *Catechism* references enhance your understanding of John and his mission?

John the Baptist is Born

Feast of John the Baptist's birth is celebrated June 24th
3rd Week of Advent covers Matthew 1:1-25
Session 6 – READ Luke 1:76-80

Catechism references to Luke 1:76
523: St. John the Baptist

Scripture references and Themes
1:76 - **The Prophet** - Lk 7:26, Mal 3:1, 4:5, Is 40:3, Mt 3:3, 11:10
1:77 – **Forgiving sins** - Mk 1:4
1:79 – **Darkness and light** - Is 9:2, Mt 4:16
1:80 – **Growth** - Lk 2:40, 2:52, Mt 3:1

In verse 76, Zechariah turns from the general praise of God in order to speak directly to his newborn son. He now knows his son fulfills the prophecies of Malachi and Isaiah; Matthew will show Jesus confirming what Zechariah says. John is the one who first gives knowledge of salvation to the people in the forgiveness of their sins. While John does not forgive sins, the One he proclaims does, and so do the men Jesus appoints with His authority as His successors (John 20:21-23).

Though Isaiah's prophecy originally concerned the Gentiles, Zechariah and Matthew both see it as also concerning the Jews. The Gentiles sit in darkness because they do not have the Scriptures. The Jews sit in darkness because they have the Scriptures but don't fully understand them. Together, Isaiah and the Gospels tell us this fullness of understanding is to be made open to all men.

John grows strong in Spirit in the desert. He prefigures Jesus not just in his preaching, but also in his life. He lives in the desert before he is manifested to Israel. Jesus will likewise be driven into the desert by the Spirit prior to the beginning of His public ministry. Both grow strong in Spirit and in favor before God. For John, this means that he grew in understanding the grace of God. For Jesus, it means He taught His human nature to obey His divine nature in all things. Though His human nature was never in rebellion against His divine nature, still it needed to be taught, and this teaching was accomplished through suffering (Heb 5:8).

As was noted in the last section, the Benedictus is an extremely important prayer in the Church. Notice the similarities and differences between Mary's and Zechariah's canticles. In the Benedictus Zechariah's words bless God, in the Magnificat Mary's very being blesses God (verses 46, 68). While the Benedictus proclaims salvation open to the Hebrews, the Magnificat speaks not only of the salvation of the Hebrews, but of the whole of humanity (verses 50, 70-73). The Benedictus shows a father blessing his son, the Magnificat shows Mary pronouncing blessings on herself (verses 48, 76-78). The Magnificat is at once more universal and much more personal than the Benedictus, directed at both Mary specifically and the whole of humanity in a way that the Benedictus is not. This is why the Benedictus is the morning prayer – it reminds us of the morning of God's covenant, the beginnings of the Old Testament, while the Magnificat's evening prayer tells us of the full scope of salvation, brought to us through the womb of the Virgin.

This is also why Luke 1:80 wonderfully caps the Benedictus. Because the Benedictus is a summary of the whole of the Old Testament and a testimony of the imminent fulfillment of everything the Old Testament pointed towards, John is likewise a living example of this imminent fulfillment. Just as the Israelites lived in the wilderness prior to being taken into the Promised Land, so John lives in the wilderness prior to the time of his work. While in the desert, God cleansed the Israelites of their idols, and John "grew and became strong in spirit." The life of the nation of Israel in the desert, the life of John in the desert, both of these are examples of how we as Christians are called to the desert, to difficulties, dry times, work, formation, study, prayer. The nation of Israel and the person we know as John the Baptist are examples to us. We as Christians are called to proclaim the way of the Lord and make straight his path. If we do this work well, then we gain what the Israelites gaining of the Promised Land foreshadowed, what John gained in his martyrdom attained – we gain heaven itself.

Questions for study:

1. Consider the emphasis the Church gives to both the Benedictus and the Magnificat. What is She trying to tell us about the Incarnation? About Mary?
2. Consider the connection between Father and child, and between God and His Bride. Given these considerations and what was discussed in the session, how do the Benedictus and Magnificat complement one another?
3. How is John's desert experience linked both to the Old Testament and to the New?
4. How did the *Catechism* paragraph enhance your understanding of John?

Jesus is Born

Celebrated on the Solemnity of Christmas and in the
Solemnity of Mary, Mother of God, January 1ˢᵗ
4th Week of Advent covers Luke 2:1-20
Session 1 – READ Luke 2:1-7

Catechism references to Luke 2:1-7
515: Mystery of Christ's Life
525: The Christmas Mystery

Scripture references and Themes
2:1 – History - Lk 3:1
2:4-5 – Bethlehem - Lk 1:27, Mi 5:2, Mt 1:18, 2:6
2:7 – Swaddling clothes - Mt 1:25, Wis 7:4-6

Luke promised us an orderly account of the events of everything that has happened, and so far he has kept his word. First, he described the annunciation of John, then the annunciation of Jesus, the birth and circumcision of John, now the birth and circumcision of Jesus. Luke's careful attention to detail and his incorporation of eyewitness testimony is further attested to by his description of the census. Sadly, our knowledge of events is not always as good as the knowledge of those who lived at the time. Two thousand years of decay have eaten many of the records which would help us know exactly when this census took place, but given Luke's love for accurately recording events, it was probably within a few years of the accepted date.

However, as is so often the case, the account of the census actually serves a two-fold purpose. First, since it is a real historical event, it helps us locate the event of the Incarnation in human history. Second, and more important, it is a sign of the work God intends to accomplish among men, "a decree went out from Caesar Augustus that the whole world should be enrolled." This is exactly what the King of Kings intended through His Incarnation – to enroll the entire world into the Kingdom of God, which is the Church. What Caesar Augustus attempts to do in a limited and human fashion, God himself will begin to establish through His grace. When this passage is read in conjunction with John 3:17, the stark contrast between human and divine work is made clear.

Through the account of the census, Luke explains where and why Joseph had to go where he did, and through this explanation, we become aware of how the prophecy in Micah concerning Bethlehem will be fulfilled. Matthew specifically quotes Micah, because he, too, recognizes that the pagan decision to take a census had brought Joseph to precisely the spot God intended him to be.

The reference to swaddling clothes in the book of Wisdom is interesting not only because of its prophecy, but also because this book is one of the books discussed in session 5 of the first week of Advent. It, along with several other books, is found only in Catholic Bibles. Martin Luther incorrectly thought that only the Jews of the second through the sixth centuries were able to accurately determine what books were properly part of Hebrew Scripture. In fact, the Jews who lived the fullness of their faith by living as Christians accepted the Wisdom of Solomon as Scripture, and this passage is one of many which demonstrates how right they were to do so. Wisdom is filled with images and commentary that conforms closely to the life and death of Christ. It is an easy read and well worth the time.

Questions for study:
1. Have you read any other ancient histories? How would you expect Luke's Gospel to stack up against them?
2. Given how pagans assisted the work of salvation, is it reasonable to expect that even pagans can be saved?
3. Read briefly through the book of Wisdom. Can you find any other chapter that recalls the life of Christ?
4. How has the *Catechism* enhanced your understanding of "mystery"?

Jesus is Born

Celebrated on the Solemnity of Christmas and in the
Solemnity of Mary, Mother of God, January 1ˢᵗ
4th Week of Advent covers Luke 2:1-20
Session 2 – READ Luke 2:8-11

Catechism references to Luke 2:8-11
333: Song of the angels 486: Conceived by the Spirit
437: Christ   525: The Christmas Mystery
448: Lord   695: Anointing and the Spirit

Scripture references and Themes
2:9 – Theme: Angels - Lk 1:11, Acts 5:19
2:11 – Theme: Jesus, Lord and Savior - Mt 1:21, Jn 4:42, Mt
16:16, Acts 2:36, 5:31; 16:16, Phil 2:11

Luke continues throughout his narrative to record details
that are important both for their historical accuracy and also for
the deeper spiritual meaning contained within them. For instance,
he emphasizes that Jesus was laid in a manger, mentioning it
three different times in ten verses (Luke 2:7, 12, 16). The word
"Beth-le-hem" means "House of Bread." A manger is an eating
trough for animals. When we read John 6:54-56, we see these
simple details really have deeper meaning. God took on flesh in
the House of Bread to be our food.

The angel appears to the shepherds as he did to Zechariah,
in the glory of the Lord, announcing our release from prison, as
in Acts. Every appearance of an angel is a message from God,
for angels are His messengers. Every word from the mouth of
God frees us from the prison of sin and death. With this angelic
announcement, several strands of Scripture are drawn together.
Just as the Church was born into the world through the power
of the Holy Spirit upon the Apostles, Jesus was born into the
world through the power of the Holy Spirit upon Mary. God
made Abraham and his descendants a Chosen People, He made
Mary and Joseph His Chosen Family. He prepared His People
throughout the whole of the Old Testament, He prepared Mary
from the moment of her conception. The salvation He pre-

pared for all mankind was known only dimly to the Chosen People, and was hidden deep within the meaning of Scripture, the salvation He prepared in His Son was known only to Mary and hidden deep within her womb. The angels' announcement to the shepherds at Christmas foreshadowed the apostles' announcement to the world at Pentecost: Mary was present at both events. What the angels proclaim here will be proclaimed in part by the Samaritan woman at the well, and will be proclaimed fully by Peter, both directly to Jesus and to those who question who Jesus is. The praise and glory sung by the shepherds will be sung in its fullness by all of us as we approach the throne of glory in heaven.

Luke is showing us that the events of history itself can be prophecy. Consider some examples. After the spirit of God moved over the waters, God created everything, including Adam and Eve, who were given the right to eat of the fruit of the trees, including the fruit of the tree of life (Gen 2:16-17). In other words, Adam and Eve, along with the whole of creation, were in a sense baptized into existence and given to eat of the fruit of the tree of life. Eating the fruit of the tree of the knowledge of good and evil was a deadly sin. They were kicked out of Paradise not just for this sin, but in order to keep them from eating of the tree of life (Gen 3:22-23). Why is this important? Recall that Jesus was hung on a tree (1 Peter 2:24). What hangs from a tree is the fruit of the tree, and the tree of the cross is the source of our life in God. Thus, the cross is the tree of life, and Jesus' flesh is its fruit. Genesis 1 through 3 foreshadow baptism and Eucharist, and Adam and Eve show us mortal sin is sufficient to keep one from the Eucharist and heaven.

This kind of foreshadowing can be found throughout the Old Testament. Noah was saved through the waters along with his family, eight persons in all (there's that "eight" number again), through the wood of the ark (reminding us of the wood of the Cross). God permitted them to eat flesh and gave to them the same command to be fruitful and multiply that had been given to Adam. As 1 Peter 3:20-21 reminds us, Noah's salvation prefigures baptism. Noah and his family could eat flesh after the Flood because they were "baptized" through the Flood, saved from a sinful world. What happened to them corresponds to our ability to partake of the Eucharist, the flesh of God, after we have been baptized and our slavery to sin has been broken. Thus it is not surprising to remember that when Moses lead his people through the waters of the Red Sea, and their slavery to the Egyptians was broken, they were given manna - bread from heaven – to eat (Exodus 16:4). Jesus will specifically make this link between manna and His own flesh in John 6. Luke makes this link later in chapter 2, tying together circumcision, another foreshadowing of baptism, and Eucharist.

Questions for study:
1. In your own words, describe how the birth of Jesus prefigures the Eucharist.
2. In your own words, describe how the Holy Family lives out salvation history in their own lives.
3. Several examples of the connection between baptism and Eucharist were given here. Can you think of any other examples in Scripture that prefigure and connect the sacraments like this?
4. Do the *Catechism* paragraphs enhance your understanding of Jesus and the Holy Spirit? If so, how?

Jesus is Born

Celebrated on the Solemnity of Christmas and in the
Solemnity of Mary, Mother of God, January 1ˢᵗ
4th Week of Advent covers Luke 2:1-20
Session 3 – READ Luke 2:12-18

Catechism **references to Luke 2:12-18**
333: Song of the angels
559: Jesus' Messianic Entrance into Jerusalem
725: Communion with Christ

Scripture references and Themes
2:12 – Signs & prophecies - 1 Sam 2:34, 2 Kings 19:29, Is 7:14
2:14 – Lord and Son - Lk 19:38, 3:22

God is in the habit of giving signs to men, so that they may know that what is happening comes from God, not just nature or pure chance. The sign of swaddling clothes is interesting primarily because of what they do to an infant. An infant in swaddling clothes cannot move hand or foot – he is completely helpless. In the same way, the liturgy swaddles the sacraments, and God appears before us voluntarily and completely helpless in the Eucharist. We can profane Him or we can worship Him through our participation in the liturgy and our love for His presence – it is our choice.

The angels announce Jesus' birth to the shepherds, inviting them to celebrate the birth of the Savior. The first king over Israel, Saul, was called a shepherd by God in 2 Sam 5:2. Ezekiel 34:23-24 shows that David was a shepherd to his people. For the Israelites, royalty were called "shepherds" because they led people as a shepherd leads his flock. When we read 1 Peter 2:9, we recall that our baptism makes us a holy nation, a royal priesthood, a people set apart. Because Jesus Christ is priest, prophet and king, our baptism into Jesus transforms each of us into priest, prophet and king. That is, *we* are kings in part because we lead others to Jesus Christ – we act as shepherds. Thus, the appearance of Jesus to the shepherds at the Incarnation prefigures the royal kingship God bestowed on us through His Resurrection. Indeed, Jesus Himself confirmed our kingship by greeting the first women he saw after the Resurrection with the royal greeting "Chairoo!" which means "Hail!" – the same greeting the angel used to Mary at the Incarnation (see week two). Jesus appears first to women because baptism makes each of us Bride to the Bridegroom (John 3:29). The summoning of the shepherds to the manger foreshadows the royal transformation accomplished in us when we are baptized and go to dine at the Mass, the Lamb's Feast. When we read Heb 1:6 in conjunction with this passage in Luke, we suddenly become aware of the myriads of angels present at Mass, kneeling at the consecration with us.

God Himself will praise His Son at his baptism and Transfiguration, and so will the people who are with Him as He enters Jerusalem. Here, the angels begin the song of praise. In this sense, we who stood with Him at the gates of Jerusalem replace the role of the angels at His birth. Similarly, we who participate in praising Him during the Mass act in concert with both the angels at His birth and with the crowds who were overjoyed to see His triumphal entry into Jerusalem.

The angels sing glory and praise to God in Luke 2:14, then the shepherds approach the manger, worship and go out into the world, proclaiming what has happened (Luke 2:17-20). We often forget that Luke 2:14 is the basis for the Gloria that is sung in Mass. If we study the Mass, we will see exactly the same order of events: we sing the Gloria, the Eucharist is consecrated, and we all go forward to worship, to take and eat. If we faithfully followed the example of Mary and the shepherds, we would receive the Eucharist, meditate, pray and ponder on it as Mary did, then go out into the world. Indeed, the very word "Mass" comes from the Latin "ite misse," which means "You are sent." The Mass is intended to remind us of not only of His death, but of the Incarnation.

The centrality of the Incarnation to the Mass and the life of the Church explains a rather peculiar thing observant visitors to a Catholic Church notice. Every Sunday during the recitation of the Nicene Creed, the whole congregation bows while praying the lines: "By the power of the Holy Spirit, He was born of the Virgin Mary and became man." However, on two days of the year, the Feast of the Annunciation and Christmas Day, the whole congregation kneels during those two lines instead of simply bowing. We kneel on those two days because we remind ourselves of the moment God took on flesh at the Annunciation and the moment God's enfleshment became known to the whole world, Christmas Day.

Questions for study:

1. Name three ways in which the birth of Jesus prefigures the Mass.
2. Connect our kingship and the shepherds at the birth of Jesus.
3. Is the Incarnation a sacrifice? How is it linked to the Mass?
4. Do you habitually bow or kneel during the lines from the Creed?
5. In Scripture, Jerusalem is sometimes used as a metaphor for heaven. Receiving Eucharist is also a participation in heaven. Given this, why is it appropriate that *Catechism* #559 references the infancy narratives?

Jesus is Born

Celebrated on the Solemnity of Christmas and in the
Solemnity of Mary, Mother of God, January 1st

4th Week of Advent covers Luke 2:1-20

Session 4 – READ Luke 2:19-20

Catechism references to Luke 2:19-20
2599: Jesus prays

Scripture references and Themes
2:19 – Mary's contemplation - Lk 2:51

Scripture twice comments on how Mary pondered the
words and actions of her Son and the events that surrounded
His life. The mark of a contemplative is the ability to drop whatever is being done and enter into prayer at a moment's notice.
Mary is what all mothers are called to be – a contemplative in the
highest sense. The daily life of a mother with her child is one of
constant interruption, of doing another's will instead of her own.
In this, Mary excelled. In this, we are all called to excel.

Many people dispute whether Jesus was actually born on
Christmas Day, but in doing so they miss an important dimen-
sion of celebrating Jesus' birth in the dead of winter. We know
that our God is a consuming fire (Deut 4:24, Heb 12:29). When
divinity took on humanity and entered a fallen world, it was,
from God's point of view, a cold day. The Son of God, dwell-
ing in the inner life of the Trinity, knows the beautiful heat of
Love. In taking on human flesh, He experienced in His own
flesh the world that does not love, this world that is so cold. In
Dante's _Inferno_, the lowest circle of Hell is a deep-freeze, for
Satan does not love. Thus, commemorating the Incarnation in
the depths of winter is absolutely appropriate, for it reminds us
of everything God gave in order to save us from our lack of
love.

It is worthwhile noting that Christmas, unlike most other
feasts of the year, has three different Masses: midnight, dawn,
and the Mass of the day. The midnight Mass signifies both the
Father's eternal begetting of His Son, which is hidden from the

eyes of man, and his birth into the world during the night and in the midst of the darkness of our sin. The dawn Mass signifies the spiritual rebirth we receive from Him through the sacraments, as Christ rises "as the day-star in our hearts." The Mass in the day signifies God becoming fully visible to us through taking on human flesh, and reminds us that the Father's eternal begetting of the Son is done in His own full light and majesty. Thus, the three Masses, each with their own readings from Scripture, teach us of the triple "birth" of Christ: in Eternity, in Time, and in the Soul. In terms of covenant, the midnight Mass can be seen as the covenant with Adam after the Fall, the promise of the Saviour made by God in Genesis 3:15, the dawn Mass is the covenant with Abraham, and the Mass of the day is that of Christ.

Questions for Study:
1. Compare the number of Catechism references using the Scriptures describing the Annunciation to the number describing the birth of Jesus. Why would the Catechism find the Scriptures surrounding the Annunciation so much richer than the Scriptures surrounding the birth of Christ?
2. Describe three ways in which God's relationship with His Chosen People prefigures Jesus' relationship with Mary.
3. Describe three ways in which Jesus' relationship with Mary lives out God's relationship with His Church.
4. Since the Mass is composed entirely from Scripture, it makes Scripture living and active. Have you ever considered studying the liturgy along with Scripture study? What benefits might this have?

The Visit of the Wise Men
Celebrated on the Solemnity of the Epiphany
Christmas Season covers Matthew 2:1-12
Session 1 – READ Matthew 2:1-6

Catechism references to Matthew 2:1-6
439: Son of David
486: The Christ in Mary's womb
528: The Epiphany

Scripture references and Themes
2:1 – Bethlehem - Lk 2:4-7, Mt 1:5
2:2 – Messianic prophecy - Num 24:17, Jer 23:5, Zech 9:9,
Mk 15:2, Jn 1:49
2:5-6 – Davidic prophecy - Mi 5:1-2, 2 Sam 5:2, Jn 7:42

Matthew's genealogy tells us Jesse lived in Bethlehem. This is where Samuel came to anoint David king of Israel. The 1 Samuel 16 story of how Samuel came to Jesse's house to anoint David's king of Israel is filled with Eucharistic references. We already know "Bethlehem" means "House of Bread." Samuel comes to the House of Bread to look for the king and offer a *eucharasis*, that is, a thanksgiving feast, and to secretly anoint a king. When he mistakenly tries to anoint the wrong son, God admonishes him not to judge by appearances, but to judge by what is in the heart, as God does. The son he anoints is the eighth son, a shepherd – we have already seen how both of these titles prefigure the Christ. So, from Samuel we learn that when we come to the House of Bread, looking for the King of Kings, we are not to judge by appearances, but to judge by the reality. If we do this, we will discover the Shepherd, the Son of the Eighth Day, through whom our *eucharisis* is made complete. Further, because we also know that Ruth, one of Jesus Gentile ancestors, came to live in Bethlehem (Ruth 1:1-19, Matt 1:5), even the Eucharist's ability to bind all people into one people, His Family, is prefigured.

Luke's infancy account is very much written from Mary's point of view. He notes Elizabeth's sterility and miraculous pregnancy, Mary's talk with the angel, how Mary and Elizabeth met and what happened after. Matthew, on the other hand, definitely writes from Joseph's point of view. Joseph is concerned with what to do about Mary, where the wise men came from and what they are up to, where the shepherds came from and what they saw. Mary orchestrates communications within the family, Joseph stands as an intermediary, protecting his family from the world. By contemplating the similarities and differences in these two accounts, we begin to understand the different roles of mother and father.

Matthew's Scripture references deal with Messianic concerns which have political relevance. Balaam, a prophet from outside Israel, prophesied this day to the pagan king, Balak, and blessed Israel instead of cursing it. Jeremiah spoke of the coming of a new and great shepherd for the people. The prophet Zechariah saw, at least in a dim way, Jesus' triumphal entry into Jerusalem. Pontius Pilate dimly understood that he faced a king, and Nathaneal knew he was king from the moment he saw Him. The wise men standing across the manger from Joseph are, like Balaam and Pontius Pilate, not from among the Chosen People, yet God grants even the pagans an opportunity to know Him and seek Him out. Matthew tells us clearly how Jesus fulfills Davidic prophecy. Because David is a sign to help us understand Jesus, what the people speak of David in 2 Samuel is a prefigurement of the truth about the Messiah, as the people of Israel themselves recognize (John 7:42).

Questions for Study:
1.   Why is it significant that Jesus was born in Bethlehem?
2.   Explain, in your own words, why Ruth and the wise men are important to the story of God Incarnate.
3.   What elements can you add to your list of how Matthew and Luke complement each other in their accounts?
4.   How could a comparison of the infancy narratives show the differences in the roles of father and mother?
5.   How did the *Catechism* references enhance your understanding of Jesus?

The Visit of the Wise Men
Celebrated on the Solemnity of the Epiphany
Christmas Season covers Matthew 2:1-12
Session 2 – READ Matthew 2:7-12

Catechism references to Matthew 2:7-12
724: Mary manifests the Son

Scripture references and Themes
2:11 – **Wise Men** - Psalm 72:10-11,15; Is 60:6, Mt 1:18, 12:46
2:12 – **Warnings** - Mt 2:22, Acts 10:22, Heb 11:7

The Gentiles are represented not only in the connection Ruth has to Bethlehem, as we saw in the last session, but also in the wise men who come seeking the Saviour. God provides them with a star to lead them to His Son. Though the star shows the wise men the general area, it does not locate for them the exact place of birth. As a result, they must ask for direction from a secular authority, King Herod. As their encounter demonstrates, trusting merely human authority is not always wise.

God established the Church and endowed it with His divine authority (John 20:21) precisely in order to guide us when we are confused or lose our way. Our "guiding lights", whether they be people or habits we rely on, can fail us, but the Church cannot. Her teachings are an unfailing guide to do what is right. This kind of unfailing guidance is prefigured in the way God touches the lives of the wise men through a dream – when they hear His warning, they change their plans. The warnings of the Church about certain habits of thought or ways of living life are likewise meant to turn us away from danger. Just as the wise men's decision to change their plans saved Jesus' life and their own, so our decisions to change our plans because of what the Church tells us can save our lives and the lives of others.

In Acts 14:16-17, Luke reminds us of the many ways in which God gives signs of His presence to us. Paul does the same in Romans 2:14-15. While Jewish shepherds were told of Jesus' birth by an angel and Simeon and Anna were told by the Holy Spirit, that is, by direct revelation from God, the Gentile Magi were informed of Jesus by a star, that is, by the evidence of the natural world. Indeed, even Old Testament Scriptures, such as Wisdom 13:1-9, remind us that the very existence of the universe is a testimony to God. Though the Gentiles who are the Magi do not know Scripture, still, careful study of the world, which was made through the Logos, brought them to Jesus. The superstition of astrology is broken by the star of Bethlehem, for through this star, the Magi come to know the God who made the stars, the heavens and the earth and all that is in them. It is true that someone can ask us how we know God exists, and we can answer simply by pointing to the natural world around us, but we must realize that this is a very difficult way to learn about God. Of all the Gentiles, only the Magi were able to discern what was happening. The Jews, who had the advantage of the Scriptures through which God reveals Himself to us, were much more prepared for the Saviour.

When we read Psalm 72:10-15, Isaiah 49:7, or Isaiah 60:6,10-13, we see how the words of God's prophets concerning the Gentiles are fulfilled here in the infancy narratives. Likewise, we see that the treatment of Solomon, David's son, prefigure the honors bestowed upon Christ. Isaiah foretold the glory that was coming to Zion, and what he speaks of is repeated in the vision John records in the Book of Revelation (Rev 21:22-27). Gold represents kingship, incense represents sacrificial offering made to God, and myrrh represents suffering. In each of these gifts, and in their sum together, we find an example of how God continually foreshadows what He is about to do.

While we don't normally think of the Incarnation this way, even at infancy, when the Son of God took the form of a slave, the beginning of the Passion of Christ can be found. The depths to which God humbled Himself in simply taking on human flesh are demonstrated to us by these gifts. The infinite God who transcends time and space chose to limit Himself by taking on human flesh and occupying a specific time, a specific place.

The earliest example of salvation coming through a vision or angelic messenger is that of Noah (Heb 11:7). Noah's salvation prefigures the salvation God provides in baptism (1 Peter 3:20-21). However, the wise men's vision is also similar both to Joseph's experience with God and the vision of Cornelius, the

God-fearing Gentile in Acts who gave praise, prayers and alms constantly. In each case, salvation awaits the men who have the visions.

Questions for Study:
1. Who do the magi represent? How do they come to their understanding of God? How does this differ from the understanding the Chosen People have? Which understanding is superior?
2. How much time do we take to study the teachings of the Church and learning to live them out in our lives?
3. The popes write encyclicals and letters to help us live an adult faith. What was the last encyclical you read?
4. From the first moments, the place where the Holy Family resided was made into a sanctuary by the wise men's offerings. What have we done as parents to make our homes a sanctuary for our children?

The Slaughter of the Innocents

Commemorated December 28th
Christmas Season covers Matthew 2:13-23
Session 3 – READ Matthew 2:13-18

Catechism **references to Matthew 2:13-18**
333: The Song of the Angels
530: The flight into Egypt

Scripture references and Themes
2:15 – First-born son in Egypt - Hos 11:1, Ex 4:22
2:18 – Rachel weeping - Jer 31:15

Just as Jesus takes upon Himself the sins of the world,
in this journey through Egypt, He began to take upon Himself,
in a certain way, the slavery of sin. Sin causes us to run in fear,
"the wicked man flees where no man pursueth" (Prov 28:1).
The Holy Family is pursued by a man steeped in sin. God allows
Himself to be driven into the land of slavery in order to join the
odyssey of His People. He walked this road once, but He walked
it in power, leading His people in a cloud of fire. Now He is
carried along the same road in complete weakness, choosing to
be helpless as a babe. Herod plays a kind of Pharoah, and Joseph a kind of Moses, only in this scenario, it is God's first-born
who will die.

"Give me children, or I shall die!" Rachel wept griev-
ously at her inability to bear children for Jacob. For a long time
she bore children for him only through her handmaid (Gen 30:1-
4). She would not be the only barren woman who lived at Ramah,
for her descendant, Hannah, Samuel's mother, also resided there
(1 Sam 1:19). However, Rachel's weeping also recalls Jacob's
sorrow at the loss of Joseph, the eldest of the two sons Rachel
eventually bore him. Because Rachel was Jacob's most loved
wife, Jacob had an immense love for Joseph, the first son she
bore him. Jacob's other sons were jealous of Jacob's love for
Joseph, and sold Joseph into slavery in Egypt, but, through his
dreams and skill at interpreting dreams, Joseph rose to be
Pharoah's right-hand man. Thus, though his brothers rejected

him, Joseph would be the son who would save Jacob's children from famine by bringing them safely into Egypt, feeding them, and caring for them. Likewise, Jesus is rejected by many of the Chosen People, but He will be the Son who saves the whole family of God by opening the way to salvation.

Matthew invokes Jeremiah because he wants us to realize that the children who died at Herod's hand were the first martyrs for Christ. These holy innocents, as Col 1:24 says, make up in their body what is lacking in the suffering of Christ, for the sake of His Body, the Church. Their blood, united to Christ by the witness of their lives, is given power by the Cross of Christ. As a result, they become God's co-workers (1 Cor 3:9). Their martyrdom for Christ is honored and transformed by God into a source of saving grace for the whole world.

Thus, it is the Jews, not the Gentiles, who are asked to be martyrs for the infant Jesus. Thomas Aquinas and Augustine together say the Holy Innocents suffered as martyrs and confessed Christ not by speaking but by dying. The children were saved for heaven through this event as surely as baptism saves children today. This is important to remember, for as Jeremiah 31:15 foretold, innocent children who witness Christ simply by their existence and who are killed simply because they exist are easily found today.

Questions for Study:

1.   How does the Church's placement of the feast of the Holy Innocents tie Christmas to Easter?
2.   What in American society most closely corresponds to the deaths of the Holy Innocents today?
3.   How is the witness the modern Holy Innocents bear to the nation similar to the witness the star bore to the magi?
4.   What are the mysteries of Jesus' infancy, according to the *Catechism* (#527-530)?

The Slaughter of the Innocents
Commemorated December 28th
Christmas Season covers Matthew 2:13-23
Session 4 – READ Matthew 2:19-23

Catechism **references to Matthew 2:19-23**
333: The Service of Angels

Scripture references and Themes
2:19 – Theme: Joseph's dreams - Mt 1:20, 2:13
2:20 – Theme: Moses' vision - Ex 4:19
2:23 – Theme: Nazareth - Is 11:1, Mt 13:54, Mk 1:9, 1:24, Lk
1:26, 2:39, 4:34, Jn 19:19

       In each case in which Joseph had cause to fear a coming problem, an angel comes to remove the fear and bring him safely to where he needed to be in order to accomplish God's will. Jesus will provide this same gift to His apostles through His physical appearances after the Resurrection (Mt 28:10). Again, we see Joseph acting in a manner akin to Moses, for both were given the same assurances of safety by God.
       The call to turn towards Christ is constant, and catches us in our daily work. Scripture shows us that it has always been so. God called Moses while shepherding (Ex 3:1), Elisha while ploughing (1 Kings 19:19-20), Amos as he looked after his herd (Amos 7:15), and the wise men as they worked. God intends our work to have meaning. Though Hosea prophesied that God would call His Son out of Egypt (Hosea 11:1), he did not say how this would occur. Joseph is not scandalized by a God who won't save Himself. Instead, Joseph does the work of a father, taking his family to Egypt without asking when he will be able to return. Likewise, upon returning, God confirms his suspicions about the safety of Judea. Though Mary is the greatest of saints, God sets Joseph up as the guardian and guide of both Mary and God. God always relies on our cooperation in order to accomplish His purpose. He placed His life on earth in the hands of His parents, Mary and Joseph. Though Joseph was not a biological parent, still, his care for Jesus made him a true parent.

God did not set Joseph up as an empty figurehead, nor does He set any one of us up to be such a thing. He intends us to expend real energy, dig into the work He has given, and make it our own through our efforts and His assistance. In this way, we show ourselves to be what baptism has made us, true children of the living God.

The prophecy described in Matthew 2:23 does not appear exactly in this form anywhere in Scripture. This is an example of the importance of oral tradition to the apostles. While Scripture is inerrant, it is not self-sufficient, that is, it does not contain everything necessary to know who God is, what He intends and how He works. Old Testament Scripture was read according to an oral tradition passed on through both the priestly and rabbinic traditions. These oral traditions were considered to be of divine origin. The Son of God chose to take on flesh at a time when oral tradition was just as important as written tradition. He never condemns oral tradition, He condemns only those traditions, oral or written, which are imposed unnecessarily by human persons (Mt 15:1-6, Mark 7:5-13). Traditions imposed by God, or those imposed necessarily by lawful human authority are perfectly acceptable. Jesus tells us this when He requires His disciples to follow the authority of the scribes and Pharisees (Mt 23:2-3). Paul re-iterates it when he requires the Thessalonians to follow all the traditions he passed on, whether by word of mouth or by letter (2 Thess 2:15).

This is why God set Scripture up the way He did. It is a puzzle that unfolds only with diligence and attention. The people of Israel knew Scripture intimately, they knew no one would know where the Messiah comes from. For this reason, Jesus presented to them an enormous mystery. They knew He was born in Bethlehem, raised in Nazareth. They thought they knew His origin. They didn't.

This is true in two ways. First, every rabbi in Israel was taught by a great rabbi before him – there was no teacher of Israel whose intellectual and spiritual forebears were unknown. Jesus was the first person to appear among them who clearly understood Scripture and God's ways, but just as clearly was never formally taught by anyone. Jesus' spiritual and intellectual origin is unknown to them. The second way in which they didn't know His origin resided, of course, in the fact that He is God. God has no origin – He is eternal. The people of Israel forgot that everyone finds his source in God. They were unable to recognize the answer to the mystery of Jesus because they consider things from man's point of view instead of from God's. To be fair, the answer is so absurd that no human person would have considered it without divine aid. Certainly no one expected God to take on human flesh. In the Incarnation, God demonstrated to us that His ways are higher than our ways, and His thoughts higher than our thoughts. If we had the majesty of God, we would never stoop to dirty ourselves with man. God, however, does not consider things in this way. We are bound by our sin, which is rooted in pride. God, however, is totally free because He is totally good. He is free to act as He does because He is not bound by the shackles of sinful pride.

God is the source of all that exists. He is Pure Existence. Sin is the distortion of that which exists, the obscuring or twisting of the good of existence. Sin and evil are the absence of a good that should be present, a good that God intended to be present, but that an angelic or human person twisted so that it is not as fully present as it should be. Thus sin is always the removal of something, and evil is always a lack of what should be. In Christ Jesus, human nature carried the uttermost infinity of Good, for God took it on. Creation carried the fullness of Good, for God dwelt within it.

Questions for Study:
1. Name three ways in which the story of Joseph prefigures the life of Christ.
2. Name three ways in which the story of the Holy Family is a story of how humanity is expected to participate in their own redemption.
3. Some of the Jewish people said Jesus could not be the Messiah, because they would not know where the Messiah came from. Why is this ironic?
4. Some people say God can sin but He chooses not to, or that God is, in a sense, limited because He cannot sin. Why are both of these ideas absurd?

Jesus is Circumcised, Mary is Purified
Celebrated on the Feast of the Presentation of the Lord
Christmas Season covers Luke 2:21-40
Session 5 – READ Luke 2:21-24

Catechism references to Luke 2:21-24
527: Jesus' circumcision
529: Presentation in the Temple
583: Jesus and the Temple

Scripture references and Themes
2:21 – Circumcision and naming - Lk 1:59, 31, Mt 1:21, 25
2:22-24 – Childbirth and circumcision - Gen 17:12, Lev 12:2-8, Ex 13:2-12

The consecration of the first-born son was closely united to the celebration of Passover, for it was at Passover that the first-born sons of the Egyptians died. Circumcision was a necessary pre-requisite to this consecration. As we have seen in previous sessions, circumcision is closely tied to baptism, while baptism is also explicitly tied to Christ's death (Rom 6:4). The death of the only Son of God is, of course, the ultimate Passover sacrifice. Thus, God wove the Scriptural themes of circumcision, consecration, Passover, and Jesus' crucifixion together into baptism, to help us understand that baptism integrates us into God's Chosen People.

Leviticus 12:2-8 describes the consequence of giving birth, ritual impurity, and how the woman is to cleanse herself and her child. The Hebrew idea of impurity is rather confusing to the modern mind, because it applies both to that which is holy and that which is unholy. For instance, touching a corpse causes defilement, but touching the sacred scrolls of the Torah likewise "soils the hands." How can this be? The reason is straightforward. When we approach the sacred, we are made conscious of our own sinfulness. Coming in contact with the sacred brings to us who are sinners the desire to be pure as the sacred is pure. As we know from Leviticus 17:11-14, blood is sacred because it is the source of life. Thus, when someone touches or is touched by blood, they are in contact with the sacred. This is why everyone who came in contact with blood, such as a woman giving birth to a child, was required to cleanse themselves – the contact with such a sacred thing, especially in such a sacred event, would properly evoke in the persons involved a desire to be pure.

Mary's offering of two turtledoves is a demonstration of the poverty of the Holy Family. Joseph's income was clearly not great. Knowing this provides some comfort to parents today who may not be able to provide for their families in the way they would like. Joseph certainly also had hopes for his family, but God permitted him to experience poverty, so that his family might have additional ways of offering their lives to the Lord. Because the dove is a sign of the Holy Spirit, one could also look upon Mary's offering as a reminder of the two books of Scripture – Old and New Testament. It also reminds us of the close connection between Mary and Scripture which will be illustrated in the sessions to come.

Some Christians point to this passage to justify their opinion that Mary was a sinner in need of purification, but the context does not support the concept. We must remember that Jesus is also circumcised in this passage, even though He has no need of circumcision in order to be joined to the family of God – He is already of the family of God, being the Son of God. Jesus is circumcised, Mary offer turtledoves, Jesus is baptized, all for the same reason. Matthew 3:15 provides the interpretive key. Jesus is baptized in order to fulfill all righteousness, that is, in order to avoid scandalizing people who do not fully understand who He is. Similarly, His circumcision and Mary's purification are also ways by which God begins to introduce Himself and His mother to the Chosen People, His family. Though already pure, she comes forward because this is God's command for all of Israel. Jesus an obedient son of God, Mary is an obedient daughter of Israel.   However, there is a further reason to come forward. In offering Jesus to God at the Temple, Mary prefigures the work of the Cross. The smallest drop of the blood of Christ is sufficient to pay for all the sins of men, past, present and future. Here at the circumcision, Christ begins the spilling of His blood. Though the payment has in a real sense been made here at the Temple in the circumcision, God wants to fully reveal Himself to us, He desires to superabundantly pay for our sins. Just as Mary willingly allows her Son to offer Himself on the Cross, so Joseph and Mary willingly begin offering Jesus to the Father here, in the Temple.

Questions for study:

1. Why would touching something holy "soil the hands" and require purification?
2. If Mary is sinless, why did she bother undergoing ritual purification?
3. Why is poverty an advantage when it comes to learning about God?
4. Given the information so far, why is it generally a good idea to avoid putting off baptism after childbirth?
5. How has the *Catechism* enhanced your understanding of Jesus?

Jesus is Circumcised, Mary is Purified

Celebrated on the Feast of the Presentation of the Lord

Christmas Season covers Luke 2:21-40

Session 6 – READ Luke 2:25-32

Catechism references to Luke 2:25-32

529: Presentation in the Temple

583: Jesus and the Temple

695: Anointing – Symbol of the Spirit

711: The Remnant

713: The Messiah's characteristics

Scripture references and Themes

2:25 – Redemption of Israel - Lk 2:38, 23:51

2:30 – Flesh sees salvation - Is 40:5, 52:10, Lk 3:6

2:32 – Light to nations - Is 42:6, 46:13, 49:6, Acts 13:47, 26:23

Simeon, Anna, and Joseph of Arimathea are all given to us as examples of Jews who followed God in righteousness. When we read other passages of Scripture which refers to "the Jews," we must recall these passages, and others like them. Each of us, through our sins, is complicit in the death of Christ; it is an offense against God to pretend the death of Christ is due solely to "the Jews."

God formed the Chosen People specifically for this moment – the Incarnation and birth of His Son. Notice that Isaiah said from the beginning that the light of salvation brought by Israel into the world would extend to the very ends of the earth. God has always intended to save all mankind. The Chosen People were His Chosen Instrument for accomplishing this. Years later, John the Baptist repeats what Isaiah prophesied and Simeon proclaimed – seeing Jesus is seeing salvation. Paul will testify to it in his first and last speeches in Acts.

The name "Jesus" means "Yahweh saves." He receives circumcision now, on the eighth day after his birth, because God will complete the work of our justification thirty-three years later on another eighth day, Easter Sunday. "Simeon" whose name means "God has heard," has prayed his whole life that he might live to witness the beginning of the redemption of man. God honors his prayers, and enlightens his mind, so that he can recognize the Messiah he has sought for so long.

Simeon's appearance is important for another reason as well, however. The Liturgy of the Hours contains yet a third prayer from the Gospel, Simeon's prayer of thanksgiving in Luke 2:29-32. This canticle is called the Nunc Dimittis; it is prayed by every person under religious vows every night immediately before bed. Since many lay Catholics also pray the Liturgy of the Hours, they also pray the Nunc Dimittis before bed. Praying the Liturgy of the Hours involves praying through many different Psalms and Scripture readings on a rotating schedule, but these three prayers, Mary's Magnificat, Zechariah's Benedictus, and Simeon's Nunc Dimittis, are the only three Scripture passages which are prayed every day without fail. Notice that, like Mary's prayer, Simeon proclaims the salvation that is made available to all peoples everywhere. Further, his canticle unites the themes found in both Mary's and Zecheriah's canticles, for he proclaims Jesus to be "a light for revelation to the Gentiles and for glory to God's people, Israel."

Questions for study:
1. Assume you have a friend or relative who reads Scripture, but doesn't understand the need for baptism. Compose a short explanation for this friend showing how circumcision, consecration, Passover, and Jesus' crucifixion are tied together in baptism.
2. We have now seen five major prayers of the Church – the Hail Mary, the Angelus, the Benedictus, the Magnificat and the Nunc Dimittis – taken directly from the first two chapters of Luke. What does this say about the Church's emphasis on Scripture? What does it say about how we should include Scripture in our prayers?
3. While many prayers of the Church are taken from Luke, none are taken from Matthew. How is the liturgy of the Church related to Mary's role in the Holy Family? How is the Church's guardianship over the deposit of Faith related to Joseph's role in the Holy Family?
4. How has the *Catechism* paragraphs on the Temple enhanced your understanding?

Jesus is Circumcised, Mary is Purified
Celebrated on the Feast of the Presentation of the Lord
Christmas Season covers Luke 2:21-40
Session 7 – READ Luke 2:33-35

***Catechism* references to Luke 2:33-35**
149: Mary's belief
575: Sign of Contradiction
587: The Stumbling Block
618: Our participation in Christ's sacrifice

Scripture references and Themes
2:34 – Swords - Lk 12:51, Is 8:14, Jn 9:39, Rom 9:33, 1 Cor 1:23, 1 Pet 2:7-8
2:35 – Knowing the heart - 1 Chron 28:9, Heb 4:12

Simeon's prophecy concerning the difficulty many would have in accepting Jesus is demonstrated constantly throughout Scripture and even to this day. The God-man who said "learn from me, for I am meek and mild" (Mt 11:29) took a whip into the Temple, called the Syro-Phoenician woman a dog (Mt 15:21-28) and did not hesitate to call the Pharisees and scribes hypocrites, blind guides, fools, and a brood of vipers. Even His disciples thought this last was a little bit too much, for Jesus' remarks had caused great offense (Mt 15:7-14, 23:33, Luke 11:37-40). However, we should remember that He healed the child of the woman He likened to a dog and saved the adulterous woman from certain death (John 8:2-11). God's treatment of man is always gentle and kind, even when we find elements of it difficult to consider so. We are called to imitate Christ in all things, to be meek and mild of heart as God considers meekness and mildness, not as man considers it.

Despite misconceptions to the contrary, we are called to live out the whole life of Christ, not just the parts we happen to like. Is it the case that polemics accomplish nothing? One could make a strong case that Christ did not think so. Is there a time for stating the truth plainly? Again, Christ seemed to do so, and rather frequently. Our propensity towards sin can, if we are not holy, turn righteous anger into self-righteous sin. However, our lack of holiness can also be present in a sinful, selfish and false humility which causes us to be silent when it would truly be more charitable speak the truth plainly. At every Mass, we ask forgiveness of our sins, both what we have done and what we have failed to do. God did all things in love, even when he spoke in seemingly unkind terms. We must likewise do all things in love.

Simeon prophesied to Mary of the sword. This phrasing is echoed in Paul's letter to the Hebrews in a most surprising context. God alone searches all thoughts and hearts, yet both Mary and Scripture reveal Christ to the nations. Through both, the thoughts of many hearts are revealed. As the gift of the turtledoves foreshadowed, Scripture, Mary, and Jesus are very closely united. God revealed Himself in part through inerrant Scripture, but He revealed Himself perfectly through this sinless woman, when the person of His Son, the Word, took on flesh.

The Church has an ancient saying, *lex orandi, lex credendi* — "as we pray, so we believe." Given the centrality of the Liturgy of the Hours to the life of the Church, the fact that the three major prayers of this liturgy are all drawn from Luke's infancy narrative demonstrates the absolute centrality of the Incarnation to our salvation. Because God took on human flesh, all humanity is joined to God. Thus, even though many Jews of Jesus' time thought prophecy was dead, Simeon and Anna demonstrate that this idea was incorrect (Luke 2:29-38). Their prophetic canticles accurately described what would, in fact, happen to the world as a result of the Incarnation.

Questions for study:
1. What three Scripture passages are prayed in the Liturgy of the Hours every day? Would you like to learn this prayer?
2. Pope John Paul II exhorted all Christians to pray this prayer regularly. Given what we have studied so far, why do you think this prayer is so important?
3. Many men do not practice the Faith because "religion is for women and children." Why might men have a serious misunderstanding of what it means to be "meek and mild"? How could this understanding be corrected? How could a close study of Matthew's first chapters assist in this effort?
4. Have *Catechism* articles on difficulties in belief been helpful?

Jesus is Circumcised, Mary is Purified
Celebrated on the Feast of the Presentation of the Lord
Christmas Season covers Luke 2:21-40
Session 8 – READ Luke 2:34-40

Catechism references to Luke 2:34-40
149: Mary's belief
575: Sign of Contradiction
587: The Stumbling Block
618: Our participation in Christ's sacrifice
711: The Remnant

Scripture references and Themes
2:36 – Widows & prophecy - Acts 21:9, Josh 19:24, 1 Tim 5:9
2:38 – Song of redemption - Is 52:9
2:39 – Nazareth - Mt 2:23
2:40 – Samson, Samuel and Jesus - Judges 13:24, 1 Sam 2:26,
Luke 1:80, 2:52

The centrality of the Incarnation points to the importance of Mary's role in our salvation. In Hebrews 4:12 and Luke
2:34-35, we saw Scripture draw a very interesting parallel between itself and Mary. Scripture twice refers to Mary holding
and contemplating her Son and the events surrounding Him in
her heart. Simeon's canticle is echoed by Paul in Hebrews, but
where Simeon speaks of Mary, Paul speaks of Scripture. Scripture tells us that both Mary and the Word of God accomplish
similar work on our hearts – through contemplation of either,
our thoughts are revealed.

Anna functions here as a female prophet. Women prophets were not unknown in Israel, as Anna and the four daughters
of Philip demonstrate. Where Scripture refers to the "enroll-
ment of widows," it is speaking of the taking of religious vows.
While women were never consecrated in the sacrament of Holy
Orders, their prayers and physical assistance were often required
in the work of the Church.

The Christian's need for prayer and contemplation is re-
affirmed by the example of Anna, an eighty-four year old widow
who fasted and prayed before God in the Temple every day,

who lived seven years in marriage and seventy-seven years outside of marriage. This spiritual preparation allowed her to recognize the Saviour. Without this preparation, would she have been able to recognize Him? It seems unlikely. After all, many people met Jesus every day, but few realized who He was, even when He was performing signs and wonders. Anna, however, recognized Him in His infancy, with no sign or wonder, star or angel, to guide her. Her prayer life was her guide. Jesus lived out a model life for us, demonstrating to everyone how we are to live in order to walk in God's ways. He constantly undertook fasting and prayer, constantly keeping His human flesh in obedience to His human and divine wills.

Fasting has great results, whether the fast be from food, drink, television, football, or something else, and whether the fast be five minutes or several days. Fasting teaches us how to control our passing impulses to do this or that, it establishes patience in us. The lack which we feel when we deliberately deny our impulses can build up in us a hunger for the presence of God. We don't have to fast from food – fasting from activities we like can build up that same hunger for God. We don't have to fast for days – a refusal to take a drink for just five minutes when we are thirsty, or a refusal to take seconds at dinner, a decision to help out in the house for five minutes during a football game – each of these are fasts. Even these small refusals to give into the impulses of our flesh can have tremendous merit, as long as we consciously join these small offerings to the perfect offering of Jesus Christ on the Cross.

Questions for study:
1.   Why is it reasonable to say that Mary and Scripture serve very similar purposes in God's plan of salvation?
2.   Christ is our Bridegroom. Given the number of sacraments, why is it significant that Anna was eighty-four and married seven years?
3.   Name a passage in the Old Testament that shows God intends to save all men, not just His Chosen People.
4.   How is Anna a good example for us today?
5.   Which *Catechism* references did you find most useful?

The Finding in the Temple
Christmas Season covers Luke 2:40-52
Session 9 – READ Luke 2:40-48

Catechism references to Luke 2:40-48
503: The Sign of Mary's Virginity
534: Finding Jesus in the Temple
583: Jesus and the Temple

Scripture references and Themes
2:41 – Passover - Ex 12:24-27, 23:15; Deut 16:1-8
2:48 – Jesus' mother and brothers - Mk 3:31-35

The finding of the child Jesus in the Temple occurs just as Passover ends. Twenty-one years from now, the risen Jesus will again be found after the Passover feast. The event recorded here at the first Passover recorded in Jesus' life reminds us in many ways of the last Passover Jesus celebrated.

The Hebrew word "to hear" also means "to obey." According to Hebrews 5:8, obedience is the only thing God learned on earth, and he learned it through suffering. He learned in the sense that He constantly chose to experience in His own human flesh the eternal obedience to the Father He already possesses from eternity. Though Jesus might appear to be disobedient to Mary and Joseph here, He is really being obedient. This paradox recalls to us another paradox which will be raised for us at the end of the Gospels: the Cross appears to be the sign of failure, as all the apostles scatter rather than face it, but it ends up being the source of triumph. In the same way, Jesus' obedience to the will of the Father is not a failure to obey Joseph or Mary. Jesus does the Father's will by teaching in the Temple. His parents want Him to obey God. Neither Joseph nor Mary tell Him to stop doing the Father's work, rather, they tell Him of their concern for Him. The moment they express this concern, He acts to alleviate it.

Mary is Jesus' biological mother, Joseph is His father through the obedience of the flesh and the authority God gives every father over the child who is in his care. For this reason, Jesus properly obeyed the real authority which Mary and Joseph exercised over Him. Yet, as is true of every mother and father, Mary and Joseph's obedience to God was the real source of their authority over their Son. The infancy narratives in Matthew and Luke demonstrate clearly their humility before God. No matter what God requested of either Mary or Joseph, either singly or together, they immediately did as God asked. Thus, it is no surprise to find that Mary's last words in Scripture are an admonition to us all, "Do whatever He tells you" (John 2:5).

So, when we that Jesus grew in wisdom and strength, we must remember that Luke refers to two things: first, he refers to the way in which Jesus' human flesh grew in strength, the way in which Jesus' human intellect grew in its ability to grasp and hold onto the things which Jesus already knew in His divine intellect, and the way in which Jesus' human will grew in its own power to constantly choose the good that his divine will had already established. Second, through his phrasing, Luke intends to remind us of one of the greatest of the Old Testament prophets. When we compare Luke 2:40 and Luke 2:52 with 1 Sam 2:26 and 1 Sam 3:1-10, we see that Luke intended his readers to read his account and remember what they saw in 1 Samuel. In 1 Samuel 16:1-13, Samuel will anoint a hidden king in Bethlehem, the House of Bread, and will die after that king is greatly persecuted and faces death (1 Sam 25:1). Samuel's life was a foreshadowing of the life of the Son of God in the flesh. Here in the infancy narratives, we likewise see the hidden King of kings, who will be anointed by the Holy Spirit at baptism, and who will be greatly persecuted, even unto death itself. Luke's reference is both a true statement, and a demonstration that Jesus fulfills everything the Old Testament hinted at.

Questions for Study:
1. Some people use this passage to "prove" Jesus does not possess the divine nature, for God does not change, but this passage says Jesus "grew." Using the information from this and previous sessions, explain in your own words why this is a misunderstanding.
2. Jesus is sometimes called "the Pontifex," which is Latin for "the Bridge" because His Person stretches out over the great chasm between human and divine nature and joins them together without mixing, intermingling or confusing the two

natures. God the Son gave power to the name "Jesus" when He did this. He does this now for all eternity. Given these facts, answer the question, "Did Jesus always know He was God"?

3. How much background is needed to answer the question above? What did you learn over the course of the last six weeks that helped you to answer this question in a way you could not answer it before?

4. Read 1 Peter 3:15. Why is it important to practice composing answers to questions like this?

5. Have any of the *Catechism* references up to this point assisted you in discussing issues of Catholic doctrine?

The Finding in the Temple
Christmas Season covers Luke 2:40-52
Session 10 – READ Luke 2:41-52

Catechism references to Luke 2:41-52
472: Human knowledge of Christ
503: The Sign of Mary's Virginity
517: Christ's life – Mystery of Redemption
531: Jesus' hidden life
534: Finding Jesus in the Temple
583: Jesus and the Temple
2196: The First Commandment
2599: Jesus prays

Scripture references and Themes
2:51 – Pondering in her heart - Lk 2:19
2:52 – John the Baptist and Samuel - Lk 1:80, 2:40, 1 Sm 2:26

This passage in Luke is meant to be a foreshadowing of the entire Gospel, especially the Crucifixion. It is here that Jesus for the first time declares himself the son of the Father. Here is the last time Luke will call the interpreters of the Mosaic law and traditions "teachers." From now on, Jesus alone will carry that title. The mantle has been lifted from the shoulders of the rabbis and priests God established among His Chosen People and is now passed to His only-begotten Son. Jesus will, in turn, allow His chosen apostles to share in this title and all of its authority, when He tells them in John 20:21, "Even as I was sent, so I send you." They passed this authority on, in turn, to the men they consecrated as their own successors (Acts 15:28, 2 Tim 1:6, Tit 2:15).

God establishes everything that happens in the world. Because it is at the Temple that the title "Teacher" is transferred to Jesus, and because Jesus was most perfectly Teacher on the Cross, all of the events surrounding this most important event will in some way echo the events of the Crucifixion. As the Holy Family journeys up to Jerusalem for the Passover, they foreshadow Christ's journey with his apostles up to Jerusalem immediately prior to his death (Luke 19:27). The Passover celebration itself is, of course, a foreshadowing of the crucifixion. After the Passover, Mary and Joseph search three days for Jesus, reminding us of the three days of loss Mary will suffer after the crucifixion before fulfilling the prophecy of John 2:20-21. When we read 1 Peter 4:6 and its description of Jesus preaching in the spirit to the dead in prison, we recall that Jesus preached first in the flesh to the rabbis in the Temple, men He would later call "white-washed tombs" (Matt 23:27). Mary's pondering of these things in her heart in Luke 2:52 foreshadows the Church's contemplation of Jesus after the Resurrection, as the apostles, the heart of the Church, prayed with Mary in the upper room (Acts 1:14). The growth of Christ the head described here prophesies the growth of His Body, the Church, described in Acts. Simeon's earlier prediction concerning the sword of sorrow that would pierce Mary's heart begins to come true here. This loss begins the preparation for a much greater loss later on.

When the shepherds came, Mary pondered. Here, she does so again. In both of these passages, we see that Mary's contemplative life was deep. She had the most intimate relationship with God any human person has ever or will ever have. Because of the richness of her relationship with God, she needed time in the silence of her heart to think on all that God had done and was doing. This contemplation, in turn, further enriched her. The Son of God, through the power of the Divine intellect and Divine will, taught His human intellect and will how to grow in wisdom. Here, the grace the Trinity gives Mary through her relationship with Him will teach her how to grow ever more deeply aware of His work in her life and in the lives of all mankind.

If we carefully study the entire Gospel of Luke, we will discover a remarkable thing: The story Luke tells begins in the Temple in Luke 1:8-9 and it ends in the Temple, in Luke 24:53. The finding in the Temple is not just a pleasant story Luke threw in to flesh out the childhood of Jesus, rather, it is a compact summary of everything he wants to tell us about Jesus, a kind of Gospel within the Gospel.

When we consider that every event and every silence in the Gospel is meant to bring us to a deeper understanding of God and how He works in our lives, the long gap in both Matthew and Luke between the infancy narratives and the adult ministry Jesus undertakes is a sign to us. By allowing this silence to work in our hearts, we begin to understand that Jesus' "hidden life," the life he lives from the age of about twelve to perhaps His thirtieth year, is a sharing in, an experience of, the ordinary hidden life of men and women throughout the world. Every day, several billion people get up, live out the day's events in small villages and towns across the face of the earth, and lay down again to that little foreshadowing of death which is sleep. Every night and every morning, we are one step closer to the death that awaits us all. When death comes to find us, we will pass through its doorway and meet our God face to face, the God who knew from before the moment of His conception what death was, and how He would deal with it. This silence is the last thing we can take from the infancy narratives, the last gift we can carry forward into the adult life through which the Gospel is made fully known.

CONCLUSION

The first Christians said "God writes the world like men write words." God authored not only the words of the Gospel, but also the events that inspired the words. Like a historical play or novel, in which the events both really happened and serve to give us moral insights on how we are to live, the whole of Scripture is an enormous morality play. It records truly historical events, yet events which "happened to them as a warning, but they were written down for our instruction, upon whom the end of the ages has come" (1 Cor 10:11). God has not finished writing this world. God's plan is not a past, finished event. It is a dynamic, living reality in which we each have a role to play. With every wailing newborn child, we hold an image of God who does not yet know God, who is lost in a world broken by sin. Each child must be led to the waters of baptism, washed and transformed into a true son or daughter, and taught the fullness of the new heritage born within through grace. Once we have been transformed by the sacraments, we must know the story of our God, and thereby our own story. Once we know it, we can live it through close connection to the sacraments and living love to those around us. The Church is our heritage, our mother, our family, the Bride who makes us her children, true children of God. Scripture is our dowry. Through her divinely guided teaching, the Church shows us, her children, how to use the wealth that tells us who we are.

Discover how to model your family on His Family!

Sex and the Sacred City
Meditations on the Theology of the Body

Already being used in high school vocation classes and for engaged couple marriage prep, marriage retreats, and adult individual and small group study, this is a book any busy Catholic can immediately use:

> "First of all, I wanted to say thanks for the preview of *Sex and the Sacred City*. I liked it so much that we're making it one of the textbooks for our Vocations class next year. What a concise, powerful reflection on Theology of the Body!"
> **-Kevin Kiefer,**
> Blessed Trinity Catholic High School

> "In just a hundred pages Steve Kellmeyer distills the rich and complex Theology of the Body. *Sex and the Sacred City* is a masterpiece of clarity. It's size, stylistic grace as well as it's logic should guarantee this book wide readership. Rarely is such a dense topic so delightfully explained and for adults as well as adolescents at that!"
> **- Al Kresta,**
> President-CEO of Ave Maria Radio

Each of the nine chapters has a study guide with questions, Scripture and Catechism references to help the reader get a basic understanding of Pope John Paul II's Theology of the Body. Discover the Eucharist's relationship to each individual Christian, the relationship between man and woman, between parents and children, and between family and the world!

Artfully Teaching the Faith

Did you know that many of the greatest medieval and Renaissance artworks were specifically intended to teach Catholic doctrines?

This short book introduces you to twelve masterpieces of Catholic history, and matches each to a doctrine of the Church. By studying the commentary along with the on-line art images, you will learn how to decipher the symbols embedded within each piece of art.

- Discover how Michelangelo depicted the three Persons of the Trinity and the dual natures of Christ by studying his Creation of Adam,
- Learn to read the symbols in the most famous Christian icon ever created,
- Discover why a masterpiece depicting Mary resting with the infant Christ on the way into Egypt is actually a foreshadowing of the Last Supper,
- Find out why a nineteenth century artist put a crumpled rug in his vision of the Annunciation.

You will quickly gain an appreciation and an appetite for discovering the Faith in the most beautiful way possible, using beauty itself! Masterpieces include:

Creation of Adam & *The Last Judgement* - Michelangelo
Incarnation - Fra Angelico
Matthew Inspired by an Angel - Guido Reni
Vierges Aux Anges - Bouguereau
Icon of the Blessed Trinity - Rublev
Transfiguration & *Disputation on the Eucharist* - Raphael
Christ Giving Peter the Keys - Perugino
Baptism of Christ & *Wedding Feast at Cana* - David
The Rest on the Flight into Egypt - David
The Incarnation - Henry Ossawa Tanner

Printed in the United States
21071LVS00001BA/39